# Clutter, Chaos & the Cure

## Or Why You Never Misplace Your Toothbrush

### Rosemary Chieppo

#### illustrated by Ernie Conte

kiwi·publishing
www.kiwipublishing.com

**Clutter, Chaos & the Cure**
Copyright © by Rosemary Chieppo, 2008

Published by: Kiwi Publishing, Inc
Post Office Box 3852
Woodbridge CT 06525
info@kiwipublishing.com
www.kiwipublishing.com
866-836-7913

ISBN   978-0-9800564-1-9
First Edition: May 2007
Second Edition: February 2008
Printed in the United States
Kiwi Publishing, Inc., Woodbridge CT

# ACKNOWLEDGEMENTS

Mara, thanks for getting me started.

Many, many thanks to my "board": Chas, Dine, Ann, Deb, Tina, and Carolee.

Ern, how many times have I said it? You're a genius!

Mikey and Liv, I love you!

# TABLE OF CONTENTS

1. Introduction     6
2. A Look at What Disorder is Costing You     9
3. I Have Not Yet Begun to Procrastinate     11
4. Sound Familiar?     15
5. Shirley, You Jest!     17
6. Rosemary's Top Five Organizing Rules     19
7. How Long Do I Really Need to Keep This?     21
8. Save or Discard?     23
9. These Are a Few of My Favorite (Organizing) Things     26
10. The (Not So) Dreaded Spring Spruce-Up     30
11. Chaos Comes Out of the Closet     33
12. Choppers, Mashers and Whisks, Oh My!     35
13. Where Do Small Household Items Go to Die?     39
14. Organized Children Is Not an Oxymoron     41
15. The Care and Feeding of College Freshmen     47
16. Basements and Garages: Prime Real Estate     51
17. The Joy of Pix (and Memorabilia)     53
18. 180 Trillion Leisure Hours Lost to Work Each Year     56
19. Eliminate Time Wasters from Your Day     61
20. Planes, Trains and Automobiles     63
21. Top-Notch Tag Sales     66
22. Make Your Next Move a Sane Move     70
23. A "Breathe-Easy" Holiday     72
24. Are You Ready for Anything?     78
25. Help! I Want to Get Off the List!     82
26. Clutter for a Cause     84
27. It's Baaack!     92

*"I've come to the conclusion that if a woman wants to lie about her age, she had better be organized about it."*

*Anonymous*

# INTRODUCTION

Do you ever misplace your toothbrush? Probably not, right? Why not? Because you always put it back in the same place when you're done with it. Your toothbrush has a "home." That's the key to organizing. You must give all of your things a "home." That, more or less, is the short answer to the organizing dilemmas so many people seem to have. But first let's define what it means to be organized.

"Your home must be so neat and clean." I hear this all the time. It's not! Being organized doesn't mean "neat and clean". It doesn't mean your home looks like something out of *Architectural Digest*. It doesn't mean rigid, and it doesn't mean perfection. I'm convinced that confusing "organized" with "perfect" keeps people from even trying to get organized in the first place. Here's my basic definition: you can find what you need when you need it. That's it, plain and simple. Life is chaotic. If you're organized, it's less so.  Lots of people are able to function well in disorganized environments. Great! If clutter and disorder are not causing them any pain they don't need this book. Those who recognize the value of an organized lifestyle and need some help achieving it do need this book.

A clean space is not necessarily an organized space. Often, when people clean, they actually create clutter, since they "stash" as they clean, tossing bags into hall closets, and stuffing things into drawers to give the appearance of "tidy." Organizing asks you to stop and think and make difficult decisions. Many people put off organizing for this very reason, since they would rather "tidy" the space than figure out where a specific item should rightfully "live."  That's rearranging, not organizing. When your home is organized it's easier to clean, because you can confidently return nomadic items to their appropriate locations, and surfaces aren't clogged with clutter. Cleaning professionals say that getting rid of excess clutter would eliminate 40 percent of the housework in an average home. Neatness can be a product of organization but organization must come first.

I was a fairly new organizer when a client said soon after meeting me, "you're not what I thought an organizer would be." When I asked what he expected, he said, "a German librarian." Guess he thought I'd arrive wearing "sensible" shoes, hair in a tight bun, ready to rap him on the knuckles if he didn't pay attention. That's so not me! I'm more of a free spirit, albeit a very organized free spirit. My six-year-old nephew says "Auntie, your hair isn't organized!" He's right; I don't have one of those "every hair in place" hairdos. (By the way, years later I had a client who actually was a librarian from Germany!)

People often say "I don't have time to get organized." I reply, "You must get organized in order to have more time." Disorganization is a time waster! Americans waste more than 9,000,000 hours each day looking for lost and misplaced items. You read that correctly: nine million hours. This amounts to a national loss of nearly $150 million per day. In addition, "crisis" purchases related to disorganization could cost as much as 15- to 20 percent of an annual budget. You know what I mean—unnecessary interest, rush and finance charges on late payments, buying duplicates of misplaced or broken items, and last minute shopping at premium prices. Like paying a lot more for a plane ticket because you bought it at the last minute. Or losing out on that $200 computer rebate because you misplaced the original receipt. Like when you know you have two cans of tuna, but can't find them because they ended up in the back of the cupboard behind the big jug of ketchup, so you have to put the baby's jacket on and strap her into the car seat so you can run out and buy the tuna because you have to make that tuna casserole now, except that it isn't on sale anymore, so you have to spend twice as much. Phew! If you're exhausted reading it, imagine actually doing it!

The word I always, always hear when a prospective client calls is "overwhelmed." By the time they call me, they're desperate. They've tried all sorts of things; nothing has worked. One of the reasons people have tried and failed to get organized is that, if they set up a system at all, it's usually too complicated. Organizing isn't rocket science. (Although, interestingly, two of my all-time most disorganized clients were science professors. Go figure!) Organizing means a place for everything and everything in its place, just like our mothers told us. One of the keys to organizing is to make any system user friendly; the simpler the better. And the easier the system, the more you'll make organizing part of everyday life. Then it will become so routine, you won't even have to think about it. You can free up the "thinking" parts of your brain for more creative purposes.

I've seen so much clutter over the years; it's made me want to lead an unfettered life. The U.S. has more malls than high schools. Americans seem to feel entitled to vast quantities of everything; they spend more time shopping than reading. Uncontrollable consumerism has become rampant in our culture. A century ago the American economist Thorstein Veblen coined the term "conspicuous consumption" to describe buying things we don't want or need to impress others. Mr. Veblen is probably rolling over in his grave. I truly believe that instead of you owning your stuff, it owns you.

Every single time you're at the store contemplating that "better," "bigger," "faster," "new," "I don't know what it is but it's on sale item," remember that you have to pay for, clean, and find a place for everything you bring into your space. One of my all-time favorite quotes is, "You never see a hearse pulling a U-Haul." Food for thought?

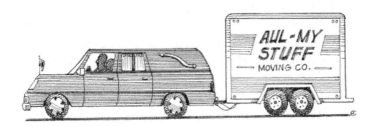

# A LOOK AT WHAT DISORDER IS COSTING YOU

- The Wall Street Journal reports that the average U.S. executive wastes six weeks per year searching for misplaced information from messy files and desks. That's one hour a day.

- Eighty percent of the clutter in most homes is a result of disorganization, not lack of space.

- White collar workers waste an average of 40 percent of their workday. Not because they aren't smart, but because they were never taught organizing skills to cope with the increasing workloads and demands.

- Realtors regard "first impression" improvements such as reorganizing rooms and de-cluttering surfaces to be one of the smartest ways to speed the sale of a home and fetch a better price; 10- to 15 percent more!

- For the past 20 years, surveys have consistently shown that managing paperwork falls in the top ten time-wasting activities of managers.

- "Crisis" purchases related to disorganization could cost as much as 15- to 20 percent of an annual budget—buying duplicates of misplaced or broken items, last minute shopping at premium prices, and unnecessary interest, rush and finance charges on late payments.

- Knowledge workers spend 50 percent of their time searching for information, leaving only the remaining 50 percent to actually use what they have found.

- According to the *San Diego Union-Tribune*, "A priceless piece of television history that legendary comedian Milton Berle feared was lost forever appears to merely have been buried under some clutter at NBC."

*"To ask how little, not how much, can I get along with. To say, 'Is it necessary?' when I am tempted to add one more accumulation to my life."*

*Anne Morrow Lindbergh*

# I HAVE NOT YET BEGUN TO PROCRASTINATE
## The Psychology of It All

When people think about getting organized they usually think in terms of physical space: closets, pantries, papers, etc. But organizing also has an emotional and mental side. What fears, insecurities, habits, and underlying issues caused the clutter? Fear of change, fear of failure, need for perfection, too much pressure, not knowing where to begin, lack of confidence? I'll do it tomorrow when the sun, the moon and the stars are in a different alignment? Are you using clutter as a protective shield, a barrier between you and the outside world? Or does it help you avoid issues or tasks you don't want to deal with? Physical clutter reflects mental clutter, so once the physical has been addressed the more subtle emotional components remain. If you really want to commit to living an organized lifestyle you need to address those pesky components.

American humorist Robert Benchley said, "Anyone can do any amount of work, provided it isn't the work he is supposed to be doing at that moment." Businessman Victor Kiam said, "Procrastination is opportunity's assassin." Postpone, delay, put off, defer, put aside. All amount to the same thing: procrastination, probably enemy number one when it comes to getting organized. University of Calgary psychologist Piers Steel, Ph.D., found that 95 percent of us report having postponement problems. People procrastinate because they perceive unpleasantness or negativity in some aspect of a task, so they avoid the discomfort through diversion. But the more you put something off the more dreaded it becomes. And thanks to the sheer variety of online distractions, it's easier than ever to procrastinate. Procrastination creates self blame and depression, which lead to more procrastination. "People who procrastinate tend to be less healthy, less wealthy, and less happy," reports Steel. What to do?

1. The best way to get something done is to begin; taking action will immediately alleviate stress. Once involved it's easier to stay with whatever you're doing.
2. Focus on specific, attainable goals. Break large jobs into smaller ones. Complete unpleasant tasks first and the rest will flow much more easily.

3. Fight indecision; people delay because they can't make up their minds.
4. Partner with someone who can help you get motivated, and promise yourself a reward upon completion.
5. Build in extra time between tasks; procrastinators often underestimate how long it takes to get things done.

Another option: wait till you're older. I love this quote: "You know you are getting old when it takes too much effort to procrastinate."

Someone asked the Dalai Lama to describe in one word the secret to living a healthy life. His answer? Routines. The word "habit" implies routine: you are repeating an action to get the result you want. Once you've formed a habit—good or bad—it can be difficult to break. Yes, old habits really do die hard. But any habit can be changed in as little as 21 days (although my client Mary Beth says it takes 100 repetitions). When you commit to replacing old habits that aren't working with new, better habits, you are faced with what feels like a daunting challenge. What to do?

1. Start very small, then build.
2. Set up easy triggers to help you remember whatever it is you want to do. Alarms, notes, rubber bands on your wrist, etc.
3. Commit to not giving up. Realize there will be setbacks; you'll mess up or forget. Don't beat yourself up. A relapse is a temporary fallback into old ways, an inevitable part of the change process. Experts refer to this as "instinctual drift," the tendency to slip back into old patterns.
4. Accept that you'll struggle for awhile until you get into the rhythm of your new habit. Sticking to your new regimen is an everyday process. If you skip it once, the tendency will be that you'll skip it again.
5. Acknowledge your accomplishments. Focus on successes and mine them for ideas on how to keep going.
6. Promise yourself a reward.

Psychologists John Jost, Dana Carney, and Sam Gosling have demonstrated that conservatives and liberals boast markedly different home and office décor. Liberals are messier than conservatives; their rooms have more clutter and more color. They have more books and their books cover a greater variety of topics. Conservatives are neater, and their rooms are cleaner, better organized, more brightly lit and more conventional. What to do?

1.  Blame your disorganization on the fact that you're a liberal.

By the way, if you want to procrastinate just a little bit longer, check out www.procrastinus.com.

*"Advertising is the art of convincing people to spend money they don't have for something they don't need."*

*Will Rogers*

# SOUND FAMILIAR?

Deb decides to wash her car. As she starts toward the garage, she notices mail on the hall table. She decides to go through the mail before washing the car. She lays her car keys down, puts the junk mail in the trash can under the table, and notices that the trash can is full. So she decides to put the bills back on the table and take out the trash first. But since she's going to be near the mailbox when she takes out the trash anyway, she may as well pay the bills first.

She takes her checkbook out from the table, and sees that there is only one check left. Her extra checks are in her desk in the den, so she goes to the desk where she finds the bottle of soda she'd been drinking. She's going to look for her checks, but first needs to push the soda aside so that she doesn't accidentally knock it over. She sees that the soda is getting warm, and decides to put it in the refrigerator to keep it cold.

As she heads toward the kitchen with the soda, a vase of flowers on the counter catches her eye—they need to be watered. She sets the soda down on the counter and discovers the reading glasses she's been searching for all morning. She decides to put them back on her desk, but first she's going to water the flowers. She sets the glasses back down on the counter, fills a container with water and suddenly spots the TV remote. Someone left it on the kitchen table. She realizes that tonight when it's time to watch TV, nobody will remember that it's on the kitchen table, so she decides to put it back in the den where it belongs, but first she'll water the flowers. She splashes some water on the flowers, but most of it spills on the floor. So she sets the remote back down on the table, gets some towels, and wipes up the spill. Then she heads down the hall trying to remember what she was planning to do.

At the end of the day, the car isn't washed, the bills aren't paid, there's a warm bottle of soda sitting on the counter, the flowers aren't watered, there's still only one check in her checkbook, she can't find the remote, can't find her glasses, and doesn't remember what she did with the car keys. Then when she tries to figure out why nothing got done today, she's really baffled because she knows she was busy all day long, and she's really tired. She realizes this is a serious problem, and she's going to try to get some help for it, but first she checks her email.

The moral of this story: it's really easy to get distracted. If the above sounds like your day, then there's a good chance you're a "zigzagger." Try setting an alarm to go off every ten minutes and, each time it sounds, be sure you're working on what you originally started working on. If you are, great! If not, stop what you're doing, and go back to your original task. It's a sure-fire way of ensuring you don't end the day with lots of incomplete tasks.

# SHIRLEY, YOU JEST!
## The Four Most Common Organizing Mistakes

I've seen these dozens of times over the years:

1.  THE PRODUCT PANACEA
    This is the mistake I see most often. My client Shirley had an entire spare room full of baskets and plastic containers. In an effort to solve her organizing woes, she bought containers, bins, baskets and various hunks of plastic to throw at the problem. Stashing items into a container does not, by some osmosis, make you organized. The product alone is not going to organize you, and just ends up turning into more clutter. That's the reason people can have tons of bins and drawers and baskets and still be disorganized. After seeing so many plastic containers of every shape and size over the years I have to agree with what Mr. McGuire said to Benjamin Braddock in *The Graduate*: "plastics."

2.  WILLY-NILLY THINKING
    Also known as Unclear Goals, but my name is catchier. The first time I meet with a client I always ask "What do we want to achieve?", and "How do you want it to look?" How can I help them get where they want to go if they don't know where they want to go? If you don't have clear goals and priorities, it will be very hard to set up any workable systems. So know what you want to accomplish. Clarity is so important if you want to solve your organizing problems.

3.  "I'LL PUT IT HERE FOR NOW"
    Scottish clergyman George Claude Lorimer said, "Putting off an easy thing makes it hard. Putting off a hard thing makes it impossible." Clutter is postponed decisions. One of the biggest mistakes you can make is creating interim spots for your belongings. You have to have a logical home for each item, rather than just plunking it down in the first place you see. If something doesn't have a place, make a place. If you put something "here" till later; later never comes. And "Someday" is not a day of the week.

4. "I DON'T HAVE ANY ROOM"

   I'm sure McMansions were spawned from these famous last words.
   Maybe that's why the size of the average new American home has
   grown about 150 to 200 square feet every few years. You actually
   have more room than you think. The problem is that most people
   aren't using their space properly; their stuff is in all the wrong
   places. Dead space can sometimes double or triple your available
   storage. And when you think you're out of space, think vertically;
   you can usually go up. But don't stack things like sweaters and
   T-shirts to alarming heights. If you actually need to get your Rolling
   Stones tongue logo tee from the bottom of the pile, that precarious
   perch is sure to topple over.

There is a solution. In order to achieve lasting change, you must dig out
of the backlog you've created over the years and replace old habits that
aren't working with new, better habits. (See Page 11).

# ROSEMARY'S TOP FIVE ORGANIZING RULES

Whether tackling a home office, sock drawer, closet, or pantry, these basic organizational principles apply.

1.  Start with small tasks so you can indulge in the victory of completion; it will motivate you to keep going. I can organize with my eyes closed and one hand tied behind my back. But I'm guessing you can't, since you're reading this book. Do whatever you need to do to psych yourself up: make sure you're not hungry, keep a drink nearby, light a candle, play some music. Whatever works for you. And don't zigzag. (See Page 15).

2.  Give your things a home at their point of use (think toothbrush). Think logically and sort by function: coffee cups and filters near the coffee pot, knives near the cutting board, pad and pencil near the phone, remote near the television. Arrange objects according to how often you use them. You use 20 percent of your things 80 percent of the time, so keep that 20 percent in prime space. Keep close at hand anything you need every day and store infrequently used things farthest away. And if you never use it, get rid of it!

3.  Group like things together: canned goods with canned goods, toys with toys, batteries with batteries, etc. Put envelopes with other stationery and office supplies, and contact lens solution with your lens case. In your closet: black pants with black pants, dresses with dresses, long sleeve blouses with long sleeve blouses, etc. When you group like things together you can see all your items at a glance. It's also a great way to take inventory; now you can actually see that you have 17 black turtlenecks and 60 AA batteries.

4.  These are so basic I fear I might be insulting your intelligence. Don't put tall things in front of short things and don't put big things on top of little things. Most people are visual; if they don't see something, it may as well not exist.

5. Organizing is an ongoing process, so once you've created a place for everything, try to return each item to its designated spot as soon as you can. We get overwhelmed when things pile up so create time every day to spend a few minutes organizing your papers, belongings, and thoughts. And no more stashing, jamming, hoarding and procrastinating!

By clearing physical clutter you'll clear the clutter in your mind. Keep your life organized and you will find more energy and clarity in every day.

# HOW LONG DO I REALLY NEED TO KEEP THIS?

You should always check with your accountant for specific guidelines, but some of the basic records retention rules are as follows:

KEEP FOR ONE MONTH
- Credit-card receipts (after checking them against monthly statements)
- Sales receipts for minor purchases
- Withdrawal and deposit slips (after checking them against monthly statements)

KEEP FOR ONE YEAR
- Paycheck stubs (except for final stub when leaving a job)*
- Monthly bank, credit-card, brokerage, mutual-fund, and retirement account statements (keep for six years if needed for tax purposes)
- Telephone and utility bills that you don't need to prove your business expenses

*Financial planners recommend keeping your final pay stub each year indefinitely to give you a handy record of your earnings and deductions.

KEEP FOR SEVEN YEARS
- W-2 and 1099 forms
- Medical records
- Tax records
- Confirmation slips for securities
- Year-end statements from credit card companies

KEEP UNTIL SOLD
- Home-improvement records and home mortgage information
- Real estate deeds
- Receipts for big-ticket items (cars, appliances, fine jewelry, art, etc.)
- Auto records (titles, registrations, repairs)

KEEP FOREVER IN A FIREPROOF
HOME SAFE OR SAFE-DEPOSIT BOX
- Birth and death certificates
- Citizenship papers and passports
- Divorce papers
- Marriage licenses
- Military records
- Social Security cards

Because some states restrict access to safe-deposit boxes when the owner dies, these should NOT be stored in a safe-deposit box:
- Powers of attorney
- Wills and trusts

Keep insurance policies (disability, medical, life, personal property, umbrella) for as long as you own the policy.

# QUESTIONS TO CONSIDER WHEN
## DECIDING WHETHER TO SAVE OR DISCARD AN ITEM

According to Dr. David Tolin, Director of the Anxiety Disorders Center at The Institute of Living in Hartford, Connecticut, different people save for different reasons, so it's important to first examine your specific reasons for saving. Then, use key questions to challenge yourself. If you tend to save because you fear letting go of something useful, try asking yourself:
- do I really need this?
- do I already have enough?
- will I really use this in the near future?
- have I used this in the last year?
- is this item in good condition?
- if I don't keep this, will I suffer financially or physically?
- do I have enough time to put this to good use?

If, on the other hand, you tend to save because you feel a sense of emotional or sentimental attachment to objects, try these:
1. is this object really important, or does it just seem important because I'm looking at it?
2. will I really honor someone's memory by saving this? Is that what the person would want?
3. is this object a cherished friend, or is it clutter that's taking up space in my home?
4. does my home really look better with this object in it, or would it look better if I got rid of some clutter?
5. if I let go of this object, how bad would I really feel? Would I feel that way forever?

If you save because holding on to things gives you a sense of safety or control, try asking:
- if I save this, am I really in control? Or am I giving up control to my possessions?
- does keeping this really make me safer? In what ways does the clutter in my home make me less safe?

- am I saving things as a way to send a message? If so, to whom? What is the message? Is it working?

According to Dr. Tolin, almost all people who clutter can benefit from asking themselves which is better for me and my clutter problem in the long run, keeping this or letting go of it?

*"Too many people spend money they haven't earned to buy things they don't want, to impress people they don't like."*

*Will Smith*

# THESE ARE A FEW OF MY
# FAVORITE (ORGANIZING) THINGS

When people discover I'm a professional organizer they usually ask me what organizing products I prefer (after saying my house must be so neat and clean). I'm all for cream colored ponies and have been known to down a crisp apple strudel from time to time but, when it comes to getting organized, here are a few of my favorite things.

1.  PLANO DURASHELF
    I rhapsodize about the DuraShelf, and if I could recommend only one product to my clients, this would be it. Most of them have this four-tier plastic shelving unit somewhere in their homes or offices. My mother bought a bunch for her basement and garage; I have three in my garage. Plastic shelving units have far outpaced traditional rust-prone metal racks in sales because they are less expensive and easier to assemble. The DuraShelf is sturdy and rust-resistant; I can assemble one in minutes without tools. I don't know how they make such a wonderful product at this incredibly low (about $20.00) price! (Sold exclusively at Lowe's).

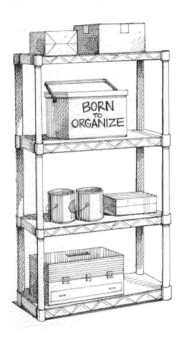

2.  E-Z FOLDZ FOLDING PLASTIC STEP STOOL
    I keep one of these in every room of my house. No more lugging a bulky folding step stool around. This stool folds down to a mere 2"; you can grab it by the handle and whisk it off wherever you need it. It easily unfolds to a secure locking position, has an unbelievable 300-pound capacity, and features a skid-resistant top and bottom. (Bed Bath & Beyond; www.spacesavers.com; 800-849-7210).

3. HELPER SHELVES/STACKING SHELVES

Getting a handle on overcrowded cupboards can be a daunting task. Helper shelves can double or triple the horizontal space of a shelf, offering more space above and below the helper shelf. They often come in a few different widths and heights. (Target, Linens 'n Things, or in specialty stores such as The Container Store). My favorites,  which are chromed steel and expandable, are at Bed Bath & Beyond (www.bedbathandbeyond.com; 800-GO-BEYOND). They come in small, medium, and large; all expand to 23 5/8".

4. MAGAZINE FILES

Magazine files are incredibly useful, and can hold a lot more than just magazines. You can also store catalogs, product/instruction manuals, etc. They are widely available in places like Target, Wal-Mart, Ikea, Kohl's, and Staples, and come in every possible permutation from basic, inexpensive cardboard to plastic, wicker, and leather. The "Blooming Bins" magazine holders at www.onlineorganizing.com are gorgeous!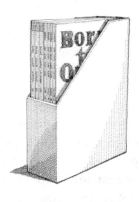

Two of my all-time favorite organizing things: shoeboxes and Ziploc bags. Need I say more?

Here are some of my favorite organizing websites:

- www.online organizing.com is a truly comprehensive web-based organizing one-stop-shop. It brings professional organizers, product manufacturers, and the general public together in one common forum. This site won the National Association of Professional Organizers (NAPO) "Organizer's Choice" award in 2003, 2004, 2005, and 2007! I use it regularly.

- www.organize.com was founded in California in 1998 as a retail store named Organize Everything. This site offers high quality products at a reasonable price. Their motto is "Clean, Neat and Easy". With an incredible array of products, it's an organizing junkie's dream.

- www.stacksandstacks.com, founded in 1984 in the San Francisco Bay Area, is a nationally recognized retail, catalog and internet company that offers over 19,000 practical, stylish and affordable products for your home, office, garden and automobile. They offer an "Ask Our Organizer" feature, and a "Clutter Control Freak" blog.

You may not be aware of *Organize* (www.organizemag.com), the first magazine dedicated solely to helping people tackle their organization needs. Professional organizer Joyce Dorny started it in 2007 when she went looking for organizing magazines and couldn't find one. It's published six times a year; I highly recommend it.

I'm astounded at how the field of organizing has mushroomed since I started my business in 1999. The National Association of Professional Organizers (NAPO) was only formed in 1985, so this hasn't been a profession for very long. If I had to choose one store I prefer for organizing products I would have to say The Container Store; you'll notice them mentioned throughout the book. The Container Store was started in 1978, seven years before NAPO was even in existence, so I've often thought that founders Kip Tindell and Garrett Boone were true visionaries. Their stores offer an eclectic mix of products devoted to helping people simplify their lives and, in an age in which customer service has gone the way of the ten-cent pack of gum, their employees offer unparalleled service. They actually seem to like working there. Heck, if I didn't already love what I do I'd try to get a job there! My only complaint: not enough stores. I always used to shop there when I lived in Boston.

To Whom It May Concern: please open a store in Connecticut.

*"Have nothing in your home
that you do not know
to be useful and believe
to be beautiful."*

*William Morris*

# THE (NOT SO) DREADED SPRING SPRUCE-UP

To me, winter is a season with very few redeeming qualities unless you ski, and I don't. But around April the days start to get longer and the air is warmer. It's time to come out of hibernation, ditch those wintry hues, and think light colors. The idea is to keep everything open and clean. Gloria's home was decidedly not open and clean. I vividly remember arriving there on a positively beautiful May morning. She didn't want to work with an organizer but her husband had given her an ultimatum: de-clutter or divorce. I walked through the front door and stared into the murk that was her living room; she was scrutinizing me as if examining a pinned butterfly. She did not want me there. The windows were covered with heavy drapes. She had about five cats and their scratching posts and toys were covering the floor. Christmas decorations, stacks of books, mounds of clothes, and shoes, shoes, and more shoes were piled everywhere. I felt like I'd fallen down the proverbial rabbit-hole. Spring is a great time to embrace the Feng Shui art of uncluttered living. You'll have less to dust, less clutter to look at, an easier time finding the things you do use, and less stress in your life. Try implementing these spruce-up tips.

1. Rid your home of all the clutter that tends to build up over the winter. Remove all knickknacks from surfaces. If a table looks too bare add just one simple item like a small bouquet of flowers or a light-colored candle. **PS:** Nothing says spring quite like a colorful display of flowers, so place them throughout the house to add color, fragrance and texture to each room.
2. Put away afghans that are draped over the backs of sofas and chairs, wintry-looking blankets, and throw pillows. Replace flannel bed linens with crisp light cotton percale and fill plastic under-the-bed storage bins with winter bedding and accessories. **PS**: Clean things before storing them.
3. Either remove rugs or replace them with lighter-colored ones. Once again, the idea is to make rooms seem more open.
4. Clean out closets. Spring is the time to put winter clothes away and bring out lighter wardrobe items. Consider donating things you haven't worn in a year since you know you'll probably never wear them again! **PS:** Don't forget to clean them first, as mentioned above.

5. Put up the shades and open the curtains and drapes so you can see all the new life unfolding outside. Wash your windows so you aren't looking through a grimy film.
6. Go big and bold with front door decorations. Remember to look at it from the vantage point of passersby to make sure it's visible and welcoming. Sweep your porch or entry area and buy lots of potted plants. **PS:** Consider buying a new welcome mat.
7. Clean out the garage and keep the door open while you work so that you can enjoy the nice weather. While you're there, store the fireplace accoutrements for the summer and give the hearth a good cleaning.
8. Do some yardwork. Replace and/or repair gardening tools, prune shrubs and young trees, prepare flowerbeds, and weed, weed, weed!
9. Clean and inspect your gas grill. You don't want any surprises when you light up a tank of propane for the first time. **PS:** You should clean the grill at the beginning and end of the grilling season.

The good news: we found the receipt Gloria had lost for a $200 pair of earrings. The bad news: after we organized just enough to placate her husband, Gloria conked out. We had just begun to scratch the surface of her clutter.

# CHAOS COMES OUT OF THE CLOSET

Remember when we were kids and thought monsters hid in closets? Now we know better, if only because there's no room! The first time I met Lucie it was love at first sight; to this day she is one of my all-time favorite clients. As soon as I saw her two gigantic closets, stuffed from floor to ceiling with forgotten and misplaced belongings, I could see she'd spent many a Saturday staggering under the weight of shopping bags. She obviously was not part of the "Buy Nothing Day" movement (traditionally held the day after Thanksgiving). Lucie felt guilty that she had lost control, and was paralyzed by the thought of reorganizing this mess. Has your closet become a monster that scares the pants off you (pun intended)? These strategies and techniques will help tame the beast.

1. Clear space, make the bed, and have a mirror nearby. This process requires trying on a lot of clothes you haven't worn in a while.
2. Take everything out, including shoes, handbags and accessories. As you remove things place them in one of four piles: "keep," "repair/clean," "give away/donate," and "throw away." Your "keep" pile should include clothes you love and feel good in. **PS**: Remember the "Eighty/Twenty Rule." Most people wear 20 percent of their clothes 80 percent of the time.
3. Discard clothes that don't fit, are worn, stained, or dated, or don't go with anything else. If you can't bear to part with your "sentimental keepers," pack and store them away. You'll still have them, but they're not taking up valuable space in your closet. In time, if you find you haven't missed them, you can kiss them goodbye!
4. Separate shirts, skirts, dresses, pants, etc. Within each group, order colors from light to dark and fabrics from light to heavy. Face all items and hangers in the same direction. Use double-hung rods for shirts and skirts; they dramatically boost storage space. The top rod should be hung at least 36 inches above the lower one.
5. Clear out the haphazard mix of plastic, wood, padded, wire, and clip hangers and start with a set of uniform ones so that clothes sit at the same level. This makes it easier to see what you have. I hate wire hangers; please don't use them! Bring them back to your dry cleaner for recycling. **PS:** Fabric can't breathe inside plastic, so don't keep clothes in dry cleaning bags.

6.  Keep longer garments to the back or sides of the closet, leaving room on the floor for shoes or other items. **PS**: An over-the-door hanging shoe rack can be useful if floor space is limited. These are also great for small accessories like hosiery and scarves.
7.  Sweaters should be stored folded so they don't stretch. If you absolutely must hang them, use padded hangers to avoid shoulder dimples. And always button them to help maintain their shape.
8.  Remember when T-shirts were plain white? Now people seem to have myriad T-shirts from every concert they've ever attended and every place they've ever visited. Fold T-shirts and divide into manageable piles. Avoid stacking them to towering heights.
9.  If you have the room, put a chest of drawers into your closet to store socks, underwear, pajamas and workout clothes. It doesn't matter what the dresser looks like; you can use a cast-off from the attic, basement or another room.
10. Store out of season items in the back of the closet or on high shelves, or another closet if you have one. Hang hooks for purses, hats and belts.
11. Leave plenty of room to get an item in or out. The goal is quality, not quantity. Heed the old saying, "Less is more."

Mission accomplished! Now when Lucie looks in her closet she sees only clothes she actually wants to wear. What a concept! To this day she calls me her "organizing angel."

# CHOPPERS, MASHERS AND WHISKS, OH MY!

This is The Big One; the busiest part of the home. Granted, I'm no cook, much to my Italian mother's dismay and embarrassment. But I often wonder if someone who actually cooks needs egg beaters, corn on the cob holders, potato mashers, cheese graters, cookie scoops, butter warmers, grapefruit knives, apple corers, veggie choppers, and grilling forks? They do? Okay; what do I know? But I wonder how our grandmothers muddled through with a knife and wooden spoon. This reminds me of my client, Rita. She took cooking classes while living in China, and her teachers, presumably good cooks, managed with one sharp knife and a wok. They were bewildered and amused that American cooks thought they needed so many gizmos and gadgets. I've organized many kitchens over the years, and I've seen some that were set up so poorly, their occupants got a complete aerobic workout just making dinner. I'm sure an entire book can be written on kitchen organizing, but I'm not the one to write that book. Instead, I'll just give you twelve tips that make sense to me.

1.  Minimize counter clutter by removing anything you don't use at least every couple of days. Is that bread maker in the corner a mute testament to that never baked perfect loaf? Relegate it, along with the crystal, deviled egg dish, and ice cream maker to the garage, pantry, or other more out-of-the-way place.
2.  If you make toast and coffee every morning, keep the coffee maker and toaster next to one another. Keep mugs near the coffeemaker and glasses near the sink. Put frequently used items on the more convenient side of the stove, sink or work surface.
3.  Use vertical space. Remember that any space you can use to hang something will free up flat space inside a cabinet. Place hooks under cabinets to hold mugs, hang a stemware rack for wine glasses, hang adhesive hooks on the inside of cabinet/pantry doors to hold small kitchen gadgets or oven mitts. Consider using wall space or a ceiling rack to hang functional items such as pots and pans.
4.  Are you "S(h)elf Motivated"? In my experience, people rarely adjust shelving, so they're stuck with lots of dead space. Take the time to adjust shelves according to your needs. Keep food visible and organized with stacking shelves. (See Page 27). Make sure to put heavy things below the counters and lighter things above them.

Position tapered glassware with every other glass upside down for the best use of space. Group together packets of sauce mixes, hot cereal packets, gravy mixes, and hot cocoa envelopes and put them into small plastic containers to avoid having them scattered all over the cabinet. **PS:** Food in tiny boxes, like Jell-O and pudding mix, fit well in clear plastic shoeboxes.

5. Use a Lazy Susan or turntables to hold oils, vinegars, spices, vitamins or medications. Check out www.spicecheckchallenge.com. This site features the McCormick Date Code Decoder, which will determine exactly when a spice, herb or blend was produced. Keep in mind the following "shelf life" guidelines for spices, herbs and seasonings: ground spices 2-3 years; whole spices 3-4 years; herbs 1-3 years; seasoning blends 1-2 years; extracts 4 years. **PS:** "Lazy Susan" made its first written appearance in a 1917 Vanity Fair advertisement for a "Revolving Server or Lazy Susan." These serving trays had been around since the 1700s; they were often tiered and called "dumbwaiters."

6. Keep two cutting boards and earmark one for meat and raw fish. Plastic boards are more hygienic than wood since you can put them in the dishwasher, but they dull knives faster. **PS:** A magnetic wall strip is preferable for knives and metal utensils. Upright knife blocks take up valuable counter space and are tough to clean; bits of food can get lodged inside.

7. Develop a lunch-making area if you have school kids or someone who carries lunch to work. Stock it with lunch boxes/bags, plastic wraps/bags, thermos, re-heatable containers, and any other lunch-making paraphernalia.

8. Make a "leftovers" list and post it on the fridge. Earmark a separate area for leftovers and use see-through containers; food gets lost and spoils if you can't see what's inside. Use square or rectangle (not round) containers; they take up less space in fridge and freezer. **PS:** A *DaysAgo* digital day counter takes away the leftover guesswork. Affix it to storage containers and it'll display the elapsed time for you. It can also be used for plant waterings, medications, beauty products, litter boxes, and a lot more. Available at www.howmanydaysago.com; The Container Store, and Whole Foods Market.

9. Create a perpetual shopping list of regularly bought foods, and arrange it in the order you shop the store. Always keep one attached to the fridge. As each item runs out, put a check mark next to it so you'll know exactly what's needed. **PS:** Both Redbook (www.redbookmag.com) and Womans Day (www.womansday.com) magazines have printable ones.

10. Keep a binder of take-out menus in your kitchen. Also keep them in your office and car to save time. Keep a phone list in your kitchen of important numbers and restaurants that deliver, and tape it inside the kitchen cabinet near your phone.

11. Keep an "Eater's Digest," aka a binder, rolodex, or box for recipes. Check out www.kraftfoods.com for an online recipe box where you can store your favorite recipes and access them anytime you want. Go to www.allrecipes.com for thousands of recipes or to look up culinary vocabulary.

12. Check out www.appliance411.com if you need appliance parts or repair help. If you're one of those hands-on types and want to repair an appliance yourself (how quaint!), they have a "Repair Manuals" section. If you've simply forgotten how to operate your appliance and you've misplaced the instructions, there's an "Owner Manuals" section. If you're in terested in factory refurbished units go to www.thegourmetdepotco.com (800-424-6783). They have repair technicians for both warranty and out-of-warranty repairs.

Bet you didn't know that November is "National Clean out Your Refrigerator" month!

*"Joy is not in things;*
*it is in us."*

Richard Wagner

# WHERE DO SMALL HOUSEHOLD ITEMS GO TO DIE?

Denise was one of my first clients. One day I asked her for some tape. Simple question, right? Denise pointed me to the top left kitchen drawer, and I opened it to find safety pins, band aids, combs, erasers, gum, lip balm, expired coupons, little thingamajigs, and something gooey which had spilled and congealed into a blob I didn't want to touch. Recognize the poor, beleaguered junk drawer? Every home has to have one, but it ends up being a household's black hole, a dumping ground for things people haven't taken the time to properly put away. Here are seven tips to turn a junk drawer into a functional, useful storage space. But let's give it a more dignified name: How about "utility drawer"?

1.  First find a convenient location. A utility drawer can be in any room in the house, but a kitchen drawer is usually ideal because it's in the heart of the home, where many people spend the majority of their time.
2.  A utility drawer should hold frequently used or emergency items. Items that might appropriately be found in the drawer include flashlights, batteries, scissors, tape, rubber bands, matches, and tape measures. **PS:** A utility drawer is not the place to keep mementos; find another place for these special items.
3.  Remove everything from the drawer and throw out dead batteries, old pieces of string, stale gum, dried-up glue, etc. This stuff belongs in the garbage. You will instantly have more space than you could imagine. Wash out the drawer so it will be dry by the time you put things back.
4.  Relocate things that belong somewhere else (and resolve to continue this practice in the future). Decks of cards should go with other games, tees to the golf bag, paper clips in the office, assorted hardware to the toolkit, etc.
5.  Sort the remaining items into piles. Group similar items together: safety pins with safety pins, rubber bands with rubber bands, etc., using whatever categories make sense to you. **PS:** Include a category for unidentified items and check with other household members for help in identifying them.

6. Organize the drawer with containers large enough to hold each pile. Empty film canisters, pill bottles, or ice cube trays are great for holding thumbtacks and other tiny items. How about old check boxes and snack-size Ziploc bags? And cutlery and utensil trays don't just have to hold silverware. **PS:** Try to stick with square or rectangular shapes to maximize drawer space.
7. Replace orderly piles in the containers you've chosen. **PS:** Extension cords are commonly found in utility drawers. Store them by winding the cord loosely and slipping them into cardboard tubes from empty paper towel rolls.

Remember to teach other household members where things belong, and let them know that the former junk drawer is now a utility drawer. It's a place to store regularly used items, not a catchall for things they don't want to bother putting away.

I never did find Denise's tape. Now that I'm older and wiser (at least on this subject), I bring my own supplies when I visit clients.

# ORGANIZED CHILDREN IS NOT AN OXYMORON

In a 25-year study, University of Michigan researchers found that kids who grew up in orderly homes stayed in school longer and then earned more money than those raised in messy ones. This implies that there is significant evidence that organization and efficiency play a role in determining academic and financial success. This certainly didn't surprise me. Organizing is an essential life skill that kids should learn as early as possible. I clearly remember John, a precocious eleven-year-old whose room needed some organizing intervention. The memory is clear not because his room was so disastrous; I'd seen a lot worse, but because his vision was so clear. Remember organizing mistake Number Two, "Willy-Nilly Thinking", on Page 17? This wasn't John's problem. Even though the room was cluttered he knew exactly how he wanted it to look, he just needed some direction. I can't remember adult clients who were so clear headed about their goals. Remember, the words "organized" and "children" do not have to be mutually exclusive. Here are twenty five tips to help your kids get organized.

## FIRST UP

1.  We assume children naturally know how to clean up and get organized, but it's something they need to be taught. Since children learn by watching their parents, make sure you behave the way you want your child to behave. If your idea of getting organized is stashing, cramming, and jamming, that's exactly what they're going to do. If you put your things in their proper place you're sending the message that organization is important. If the entire house is orderly it will be easier for your child to remain orderly.
2.  When planning an organizing system for your kids, you should first consult the experts — them! Together, you and your children should determine how things should be stored, when and where items are used most frequently, etc. By including them in the planning process, your kids will feel more inclined to keep the system in good, working order. No matter what solutions you decide on, make sure that your child understands that this is her own space, where her stuff should be kept at all times. Creating this sense of ownership will help her stick to the storage plan. **PS:** Remember to reward and motivate rather than punish, ie WHEN your toys are picked up THEN you can watch a movie (or whatever).

## TOYS, BOOKS AND PUZZLES

This stuff seems to consume every area of a home. Don't forget often-overlooked areas under the bed and over the door. Maximize all of your vertical space and make sure shelves are at kid height. Store things your child doesn't need to access regularly on top shelves.

3. Categorizing and keeping like-things together should be taught between the ages of three and six. Toys should be organized by category (cars and trucks together, dolls together, action figures together, specific types of games together, etc) in see-through containers, not in a toy chest. If a child has to search for a toy in a chest, he'll probably dump out the entire box to find it. **PS:** A tiered, expandable pantry organizer is a wonderful showcase for small cars, toy motorcycles or Lego creations.

4. Depending on the child's age, put a removable label with words or pictures on containers to help them immediately identify what's inside. Be sure to print in neat (mostly) lower case letters, ie small round toys, balls, crayons, costumes, etc. You'll be sorting by kind, size, and shape. Lids are usually too much for kids to deal with, so get containers without lids or store the lids elsewhere for when the kids aren't using the containers anymore. **PS:** The Company Store's *Stackable Cube Storage Collection* is a great place to stash toys, stuffed animals, trucks and blocks. The cubes are available with or without doors, and can be stacked or un-stacked for multiple storage options. (www.thecompanystore.com; 800-323-8000).

5. Shoeboxes, photo boxes, and plastic frozen food containers can be used to hold stamps and baseball card collections. The Container Store has a case that holds up to 800 cards. **PS:** Tackle boxes come in lots of sizes and are great for small items like marbles and beads.

6. Limit toys to certain areas of the home: inside toys, outside toys, upstairs toys, downstairs toys. This can be a safety factor, since all toys that can be thrown (balls, Frisbees) are best used outdoors. Paper items such as books or paper dolls are indoor toys. If you have a two-story home, set a rule that upstairs toys are not to be dragged downstairs; they stay in the bedroom or playroom. Downstairs push or riding toys must stay downstairs and off the steps.

7. Too many toys, books and puzzles? That's a rhetorical question, since most kids have way too many toys, books and puzzles! The

more stuff a child has the harder it is to organize, so pack some away. When boredom sets in you can switch to the stored items, which will seem like new again. When your children receive new toys, help them select old ones to clean up and donate to a local charity. Children love the feeling of helping others.

8. Check out books from the library, and buy only the ones your children really love. Why spend money on books they'll never read? Don't sign up for "Whatever of the Month Clubs". If you forget to tell them you don't want that month's selection, your kids end up with books and toys they didn't choose, don't want, and don't play with.

## ARTWORK

You love your kid's art and she needs to celebrate her artistic endeavors, right? But artwork can start to resemble a bug infestation.

9. Hang a clothesline along one wall of the child's room and use clothespins to display artwork. Rotation is easy and clothespins won't damage the artwork. Once it's been displayed, if the child can't part with it, use clear under bed containers for longer-term storage. **PS:** See if you can entice your favorite pizza joint to part with some clean pizza cartons. They make for great under bed storage.

10. Crayons, markers and pencils can have a place of their own in a sturdy wooden carryall that your child can tote around. KidKraft makes a nice one that comes in lots of colors. (www.kidkraft.com; 877-KIDKRAFT).

11. At the end of every month have your child pose for a picture surrounded by that month's artwork. Create a special album and add the pictures to document projects over the year(s). **PS:** School-folio (www.schoolfolio.com; 800-288-4195) offers all-in-one storage solutions that organize and protect art, schoolwork, report cards, class photos and other keepsakes from pre-school to 12th grade.

12. When you run out of room on the fridge, lay artwork on the kitchen table and cover with a clear plastic tablecloth held tight with picnic-table clips.

## CLOTHING

13. Hang as much as possible. If clothes are in a folded pile or in a drawer, kids are more likely to wear what's on top rather than looking through the pile. Install closet shelving they can easily reach and use lots of hooks. I like the Container Store's Elfa shelving system because it's totally adjustable. As the kids grow taller you just snap out the shelves and snap them in higher up on the tracks. Or install an adjustable shower curtain rod in the closet. As the kids grow you can keep adjusting the rod to fit their reach. **PS:** Lillian Vernon's *School Days Closet Organizer* has brightly labeled slots for a week's worth of outfits. And it helps teach the days of the week. (www.lillianvernon.com; 800-901-9402).

14. If you do use drawers, put pictures of shirts, pants, underwear and other clothing on the proper drawers. Put shoe boxes without lids in drawers to help keep clothes from getting jumbled. Socks in one box, underwear in another, etc.

15. I use over-the-door shoe bags for lots of things. How about using one for small items like socks, mittens, and earmuffs?

Make sure to help them keep drawers and closets at a point where they can easily fit their clothes and other belongings into them without pushing or shoving.

## LAUNDRY

16. Every kid needs a hamper — some place to throw dirty laundry. Put a designated box or basket in each child's room. Make a rule: dirty clothes that are not in the hamper don't get washed! To simplify laundry, assign a signature color to each child for towels, sheets and blankets.

17. Some families have a laundry basket in every room so that the kids (and grownups) don't have to go to a central location to deposit dirty clothes. Another advantage of this is that you can choose to wash every child's clothes separately, so that you don't have to sort them later. Even if you don't do that, it's pretty easy to walk around the rooms when you plan to wash and, for example, pick up all the whites from the different baskets. **PS:** Sock Locks plastic rings hold pairs of socks together in the wash. (www.sock-locks.com; 973-224-0245).

18. Try "dot coding" all kid clothes. Use a black laundry marker and put dots on the label of every piece of clothing. Kid #1 has one dot, kid #2 has two dots, and so on. This means that everybody, even toddlers, can sort clothes. When a kid outgrows something, put a new dot on it before it goes into the dirty clothes hamper; next time it will be put in the next one's closet.

## STUFFED ANIMALS
19. Too many stuffed toys making a mess? Here's that over-the-door shoe bag again! Give the smaller toys a sweet place to rest by placing them in a shoe bag on the inside of a closet door. Your children will enjoy seeing their heads popping over the top of the sleeves whenever they open their closets.
20. Hang a toy hammock in your child's room and place the overflow of stuffed animals there. Sling it low enough so your child can reach it. If the child has outgrown them, but isn't ready to part with them, hang the hammock way up in the corner of the ceiling. The toys can still be seen but are out of the way. **PS:** The Container Store's *Calypso Toy Trolley* is a cheery catchall on wheels that's perfect for corralling stuffed animals and lots of other things. (www.containerstore.com; 1-888-CONTAIN).

## SCHOOLWORK
Proponents of the Montessori teaching method have worked for more than 100 years with children as young as 18 months to introduce them to sequential, organized behavior. What location is to real estate, organization is to school work!

21. Organizing a study area for your children may be the most important thing you do for them. Make sure they have a quiet, well-lit place to do homework. Don't let them study in front of the television or in an area where they will be distracted. Eliminate the chronic search for rulers, paper and pencils by keeping a bin of study supplies stored in the designated study area. **PS:** Set up consistent study/homework times. Kids need routines!
22. Teach kids to keep a notebook with them to write down all assignments and tasks for every class along with their due dates. Since kids often don't realize how long a task can take from start to finish, help them learn to manage time by listing all their

responsibilities in that notebook: chores, homework, soccer practice, etc., and how much time each will take.

23. Prepare each evening for the next day. Pick out clothes and shoes, pack lunches, set out breakfast and place backpacks by the door, ready to go. Make an out-the-door checklist. Note everything they need to take to school and post it on the door.

24. Place a rack near the door for outerwear and a shelf or mat for shoes. Have kids deposit their coats, hats, gloves and shoes upon entering. Have them sort through their backpacks and organize all materials and books. Provide a designated place where they can place anything for parents' review. This will avoid lost or neglected homework assignments, misplaced papers and school notices. **PS:** Create a filing system for school papers; there will be lots of paper! Make copies of frequently used parental release forms/permission slips.

For more information on this subject, pick up *The Organized Student: Teaching Children the Skills for Success in School and Beyond,* by Donna Goldberg and Jennifer Zwiebel.

## MAINTENANCE

25. The best way to make sure your child sticks to a system is to make it fun. Make it a game. Close your eyes and count to ten while your child puts things away. Or set a timer and play "Beat the Clock." Make it a race to see if stuff can be put away before the buzzer goes off. If done in time they get a reward. Whatever you do, by helping reinforce the importance of putting things away, you'll help create a healthy routine for your child. Children thrive and depend on routine.

These twenty five tips will let your kids experience the freedom and ease organizing brings. Children who are organized feel good about themselves and have an easier time managing life skills.

# THE CARE AND FEEDING OF COLLEGE FRESHMEN

Kids are priceless, right? In 2006, the U.S. Department of Agriculture estimated that the average upper-middle-class family spends a whopping $182,000 on each child by age 17. Ouch! Chip, one of my favorite clients, was ready for his firstborn (of five!) to fly the coop, and asked me to help prepare for the sendoff. There are definite rites of passage in society and going away to school for the first time is a big one. Suddenly, the child is no longer a child, but someone who is expected to become educated and employable and make her way in the world. These tips will make the transition to college life much easier.

## DORM ROOMS

1. How do you fit clothes, books, computer and other necessities into a space no bigger than a prison cell? Not easily. If possible, check out new accommodations prior to packing and find out in advance what's supplied. Many dorms have suggested floor plans to maximize space. Store as much as possible under the bed and, if necessary, purchase bed risers (about $10) to raise the bed off the floor a few inches to allow containers to fit. **PS:** Most dorm beds are extra long so find this out before purchasing sheets and other bedding.
2. When packing for college, less is more. Bring only necessities— bedding, toiletries, computer, school supplies, clothing and favorite music. If something is left behind, almost every city in America has something akin to a Wal-Mart.
3. Most students will have a roommate. Try to contact the new roomie before getting to school. If possible, coordinate to avoid duplication of items such as television, fridge, and ironing board. **PS:** Check with the college to avoid bringing items that may not be allowed such as microwaves, toaster ovens, space heaters, etc.
4. Make the most of allotted space by hanging clear pockets inside closet doors to store socks, gloves, hats, etc. Use wall space for shelving or memo boards. Attach hanging pockets to the end of the bed. **PS:** Suitcases can store clothing and extra linens.

5. A laptop takes up less space than a desktop computer and provides portability for working on assignments away from a dorm room. Stereos, televisions, electronic games, etc. should be compact. Label these items with name and record the serial numbers in the event of theft.

## FINANCES

6. Have an open family discussion about money and set a realistic budget. Open a checking account at a bank branch near campus. Students should get some coaching on how to maintain a checkbook and parents should review the first banking statements. Without these skills students may end up paying stiff fees for bounced checks or an overdrawn account.
7. Three-fourths of undergraduates have a credit card in their name. Freshmen should start handling their own plastic early (the lower the credit limit, the better) to build a credit rating and the budgeting skills they'll need when they hit the real world. Statements should be sent to parents for monitoring, not payment. **PS:** Today's college students graduate with an average of $3,000 in credit card debt.

## CLOTHING/LAUNDRY

8. Get the scoop on the college town's year-round forecast and only take clothing suited to the current season. Pack what's needed for the first quarter or semester, then get additional items over the Thanksgiving or Christmas holiday. Layer clothing to suit the weather. Make sure to have enough underwear to last at least two weeks or until laundry day.
9. Students should be trained to handle laundry well before school starts. The first week of classes is not the time to find out what a red sock does to white shirts. Start dorm life with a folding laundry bag or pop-up mesh laundry basket (plastic laundry baskets take up too much space), a couple of rolls of quarters, liquid detergent, and written instructions, maybe even laminated, on how to do laundry. **PS:** Neutral towels and sheets are best, in case loads aren't separated too carefully.

## HEALTH/SAFETY

10. Every dorm room should have these basic safety items: a fully-stocked first aid kit, including thermometer, aspirin; copies of prescriptions; a flashlight with fresh batteries; and a surge protector or uninterruptible power supply. Freshmen should know where the student health center is and what services are available. Parents should check their health insurance policy to make sure the child is covered. **PS:** Kids need a list of phone numbers and contact information for friends, family members and emergency contacts. Parents should get the new roommate's cell phone number.

My last words to Chip's son: don't sign up for an 8:00AM class. And call your parents!

*"Simplicity, simplicity, simplicity! I say, let your affairs be as two or three, and not a hundred or a thousand. Simplify, simplify."*

*Henry David Thoreau*

# BASEMENTS AND GARAGES: PRIME REAL ESTATE

Nobody ever seems to have enough storage space, right? Even though I had seen lots of clutter by the time Gladys ushered me into her basement and garage on a bright spring day, I was taken aback. I might have run screaming for the exit but was stuck in a maze of lawn chairs, garden tools, Christmas decorations, pots and pans, mattresses, coats, and knick-knacks. Her garage and basement looked more like a modern-day elephant burial ground than part of someone's home, and was a major irritation and source of embarrassment for Gladys. Capitalism needs us to want what we don't have and, by golly, Gladys was a Capitalist! According to a study by the U.S. Department of Energy, 25 percent of people with two-car garages didn't park any cars in them, and 32 percent parked only one. It's safe to say that Gladys was squarely in that 25 percent! It doesn't have to be that way. Consider these nine tips:

1.  View basements and garages as rooms and plan how you're going to use the space; visualize how you'd like it to look and feel. Grouping like things together is one of the most basic organizing principles. So create "zones"; a gardening zone, a camping zone, a recycling zone, etc. This makes for a logical system. **PS:** Always label!
2.  Use indoor/outdoor carpeting in a finished basement. It dries easily and doesn't mold like a regular carpet. **PS:** Use a dehumidifier to keep carpeting dry.
3.  Make sure all your equipment is clean and maintained before storing. Mud or dirt can cause rust, mildew or deterioration. **PS:** Donate or throw away before you store; why make room for items that need replacement?
4.  Your storage area should be dry and ventilated. Wrap items appropriately. Lawn furniture cushions should be thoroughly dry before storing and then placed loosely in a nylon bag or plastic storage bin to keep them dust free.
5.  Don't keep anything directly on a basement floor in case of water damage. Cement blocks with wood pieces create instant shelves. Better yet, use clear plastic bins. You can see what's inside and the bins protect from water damage. **PS:** If you absolutely must store something on the floor, line the box with plastic.

6. Don't forget valuable wall space. Hang pegboards and hooks, add shelving, and put a sturdy utility shelf unit (See Page 26).
7. Place gardening tools—rakes, shovels, hoes, etc.—inside a sturdy trash barrel with wheels. Hang small tools around the rim. When it's time to garden just roll the can to wherever you want to work.
   **PS:** Trash barrels are also great for hockey sticks, bats, balls, etc.
8. Store the lawn mower in a ventilated area, away from flammable items. **PS:** Get both the leaf and snow blowers serviced and ready for fall and winter.
9. Turn a plastic wading pool into a holding bin for inflatable toys, beach totes, and other seasonal accessories. **PS:** Drawers from old furniture and empty luggage are great for storing. The luggage is going to be sitting there anyway; why not put it to good use?

I organized the garage and basement and, soon after, Gladys moved! Oh well...

# THE JOY OF PIX (AND MEMORABILIA)

Remember that romantic trip to Paris in 1991? Your best friend's wedding in 1993? Bet you took lots of photos, right? Still have your fifth grade report card, the one where Miss Crabtree said you played well with others? You've probably got lots of handwritten notes and ticket stubs, too. Where is all this stuff? People routinely list photos and memorabilia among their most prized possessions but, if you're like most of my clients, they are shoved into bags, drawers, or shoeboxes under the holiday decorations in your garage, attic, or basement. Creating a home for them just never seems to rise to the top of anyone's to-do list. Digital camera sales surpassed 35mm-camera sales in 2003, but what to do with those pre-digital photos? If the thought of organizing them is frustrating and overwhelming, these tips will help.

1.  First, a few don'ts:
    - don't laminate memorabilia; heat from laminating machines can cause items to age more quickly
    - don't use rubber cement, tape or glue in albums; only use acid-free adhesives
    - don't store photos/memorabilia with newspaper; acid from the newspaper can damage your keepsakes
2.  Decide if you'll accomplish more in a marathon organizing session or regularly scheduled mini sessions. If you opt for the marathon, plan breaks about every thirty minutes. Designate and clear a space where you can work comfortably. The kitchen table is usually good; it's a good height and you'll be able to spread everything out.
3.  Albums or boxes? A photo box is the easiest option, but it's more difficult to show your pictures when they're in a box. Photo albums are more user-friendly and photos can be arranged along with those ticket stubs and handwritten notes, but putting an album together is more time consuming. Whichever you choose, make sure they have acid-free pages or lining to preserve the life of your photographs. Check out www.exposuresonline.com (800-222-4947) for stylish storage options and handcrafted leather albums and scrapbooks. **PS:** If you're really ambitious and creative try scrapbooking, which involves details like stickers, artwork, and captions.
4.  Throw away photos that are dark, blurry, or of people you don't recognize. If you've got several photos of the same topic, choose one

or two of the best and purge the rest. Put aside photos to frame or send to friends and family. **PS:** If you agonize over getting rid of dupes put them in a separate album and gift it to a friend/family member.

5. Want to keep negatives? Take a look at www.mvconservation.com (646-645-1465) for envelopes, sleeves and storage boxes.

6. Figure out how you'd like to organize your photos. By event (all vacations in one album, all weddings in one box)? Chronologically? By person (Olivia's Photo Box, Dad's Photo Album)? Create a simple, uncomplicated system. Take the time to jot down a ballpark date and any quick memories or quotes that come to mind; photos will have more meaning if you know the story behind them. Sort into appropriate piles and start filling albums/boxes. **PS:** Use an acid-free photo pen.

7. That was easy! Not easy enough? If you simply don't have the time or inclination to do it all yourself, www.photoworks.com (800-746-8696), or www.kolo.com (888-636-5656) will turn your photos into a professionally bound hardcover book.

8. Boxes and albums too mundane? Another way to showcase your precious photos is to use them to make mugs, calendars, mouse pads, tote bags, coasters, T-shirts, and just about anything else you never thought of. Turn a favorite photo into a deck of playing cards at www.kodakgallery.com (800-360-9098). Or put a photo on real U.S. postage stamps at www.photostamps.com. You can turn photos into large framed canvas prints, purses, ceramic tiles, or even end tables at www.photowow.com (800-453-9333). Want a blanket, pillow, or towel emblazoned with your beloved's visage? Go to www.treasureknit.com. Customize a lampshade or sterling silver pendant at www.maryjaneappel.com (202-363-4239).

9. Wish you could email photos along with the stories behind them? Thanks to www.beta.yodio.com you can combine photos with sound files to create audio postcards. Just upload photos, then call Yodio's number (877-MYYODIO) and start talking to create accompanying audio (or record your own MP3 file and upload that).

Now that your photos/memorabilia finally have a good home, protect them from hazards like excessive heat, light and humidity. In other words, don't stash them back in the garage, attic or basement!

*"Three rules of work:*
*out of clutter find*
*simplicity; from discord find*
*harmony; in the*
*middle of difficulty lies*
*opportunity."*

*Albert Einstein*

# 180 TRILLION LEISURE
# HOURS LOST TO WORK EACH YEAR

That'll keep you up at night! It's true, at least according to Boston University's School of Lifestyle Management. So until you win the lottery and tell your boss to take a hike, why not make your workplace work for you? I remember the first time I went to Anne's office. She was exasperated, and it took me about four tenths of a second to see why. I was confronted with precarious Leaning Towers of Paper, uncapped pens, old receipts, CDs scattered hither and yon, and paper cups with an unearthly mix of coffee, cigarette butts, and a hint of something green just starting to appear. Instead of an efficient, functional space her office was a megadisaster! Office clutter is not only unattractive, it interferes with productivity. Anne admitted it was nearly impossible for her to think straight in such a chaotic situation. So whether you work in a Fortune 500 company, a corner of your kitchen, or a cubbyhole under the front stairway, these sixteen tips can be adapted to work wherever you work.

1. Think ergonomically. Put pens, scissors, tape, paper clips, filing cabinets, and all frequently used materials within arms' reach of your desk chair. If you have to get up to put something away, chances are you won't. **PS:** You should also have instant access to any equipment you use frequently.
2. De-clutter your desk. Keep only items that relate to current projects. A clear desk means a clear mind, and a clear mind has vision and perspective. Always leave your desk clear when you finish working and place tomorrow's top priority at the center so you'll start your day focused. **PS:** Clear your desk top of personal mementos. Hang on the walls or place on shelves. Give yourself space to work, without distractions.
3. Keep desk items on the preferred side. Whichever hand you use most often is your preferred side. The only exception is the telephone: keep it on the opposite of the preferred side so you can use your preferred hand to take notes. **PS:** Use a portable phone or one with a long enough cord so that you can reach all of your files and necessary items while on the phone.
4. Make phone calls more productive. Say, "I only have five minutes to talk." Outline your calls: "I'd like to discuss these two possible

solutions to problem Z . . ." If you have to leave a voice mail, slowly state your name, company, when you are calling, a brief message about your purpose, and a telephone number at the beginning and again at the end of your message. If there's another extension of someone as an alternate contact, leave his/her name and extension as well. When completing a phone call, write down your next action relating to the call. Do you need to make another call or mail something? If you can't do it now, write it down. **PS:** A planned call takes seven minutes; an unplanned one takes twelve.

5. Create one good calendar system and have it with you at all times. The biggest mistake people make when using planning calendars is to have one for personal, another for the office, and yet another for the family. Keep personal, professional and family items on one calendar. It will eliminate scheduling conflicts.

6. Don't be an "email slave." Set aside two or three times a day to check it, and delete as you go. **PS:** Place your contact information in all your email replies. Include phone number and extension.

7. Schedule meetings with both beginning and ending times. People are more "to-the-point" when they are up against a deadline. Provide an agenda to stay focused and decrease wasted time. Take a highlighter to meetings. As you make notes, highlight anything which will require action on your part. **PS:** Keep a file for regular meetings you attend. If you have a weekly meeting with your boss, fill a file with items to review.

8. Does your office resemble Grand Central Station? The average office worker is interrupted every three minutes, according to researchers at the School of Information and Computer Science at UC-Irvine. A related study showed that it can take 10 to 20 minutes to regain your concentration after each interruption. Whether an office or cubicle dweller, reduce these interruptions by positioning your desk so passersby will not be able to catch your eye, thus avoiding unnecessary conversation. Recognize distractions and try to eliminate them; they come in a zillion forms and keep you from the task at hand. Understand the real issue: you're allowing yourself to avoid a task by giving in to distractions. Then the next time you're tempted by a distraction, STOP and focus on your priorities

9. Be realistic about how long things take and allow for the unexpected. Plan 60 percent of your time and allow 40 percent to accommodate

unexpected delays/interruptions. Learn to estimate how long a task will take and, at first, double your "guesstimate."

10. Do first the thing you like least. This is an excellent timesaving habit to get into. Most people waste far too much time and energy thinking about dreaded tasks rather than actually doing them. Get the most disliked jobs out of the way first, and you'll get a great sense of accomplishment. Plus, you'll be able to enjoy the rest of the day, knowing your worst task is out of the way.

11. Don't over commit yourself. Getting overcommitted is a huge time trap. If this is a frequent problem, either you haven't learned to say "no," or you aren't accurately estimating how long it will take to complete certain tasks. Over scheduling adds unwanted stress to life; always check your calendar before you agree to do anything more.

12. Multitasking is overrated! Performance declines — and stress rises — with the number of tasks juggled. A certain amount of multitasking could lead to greater efficiency, but too much produces declining performance. Instead, devote chunks of time to individual tasks and focus on each solely and completely. **PS:** The term multitasking was originally coined to describe what a computer does during the microseconds between keystrokes.

13. Delegate. Invest time teaching others how to do a specific task. When you delegate, you instantly increase time you have available — and you help others learn new skills. First, determine who can best handle the task. Then thoroughly explain the job, your expectations, deadlines and how you'll monitor progress. Put these points in writing then ask him/her to summarize the assignment so you'll know you've clearly communicated what's been delegated.

14. Batch. Don't mail, fax, copy, or stamp one item at a time. Set up a regular time toward the end of the day to prepare all outgoing packages/correspondence, with the exception of emergency messages. **PS:** The average office worker makes about 61 trips per week to the fax machine, copier, and printer.

15. If you're on the road a lot, put staplers, pens and pencils, paper clips, Post-it Notes, file folders, etc., in a briefcase, and leave it in your car. If you travel regularly, keep a bag stocked with toothpaste, toiletries, and other personal travel items. **PS:** In the 1890s, the double-oval design paper clip was first produced by the British company Gem Manufacturing. In 1980, 3M introduced the first Post-it Note nationally.

16. Create forms/templates for regularly used documents: contracts, proposals, expense reports, personalized fax cover sheets, etc. Make copies and keep them nearby.

On December 10, 1948 the General Assembly of the United Nations adopted and proclaimed the Universal Declaration of Human Rights. Article 24 states that, *"Everyone has the right to rest and leisure, including reasonable limitation of working hours and periodic holidays with pay."*

*"Half our life is spent trying to find something to do with the time we have rushed through life trying to save."*

Will Rogers

# ELIMINATE TIME-WASTERS FROM YOUR DAY

How are you? *"Busy."* How's work? *"Busy."* How's the family? *"Busy."* We hear it again and again and again. Many metaphors have been used to describe life's brevity. Victor Hugo said, "Short as life is, we make it still shorter by the careless waste of time." Benjamin Franklin said, "Lost time is never found again." The writer Louis E. Boone said, "I definitely am going to take a course on time management… just as soon as I can work it into my schedule." Remember "Sound Familiar?" on Page 15? I have had so many clients who suffer from "zigzag" tendencies. There are only 24 hours in a day, so how to wisely use our daily allotment of 1,440 minutes as they steadily tick away? Here are twelve simple tips to follow for better time management.

1. Plan your days. You'll accomplish more when you know what you want to do. Set goals that are specific, realistic and achievable.
2. Learn to delegate. Is there someone who can do it faster? Is there someone who can do it better? Is there someone who can do it well enough?
3. We waste time looking for lost items, digging through clutter, and being distracted by having to go elsewhere to retrieve an item. Keep things where you use them. It's the number one de-cluttering, time-saving, and organizing rule.
4. Do everything you can during off-hours. Steer clear of the bank or post office on Fridays; avoid driving during commuting hours or school dismissals; try to book the first appointment of the day with your doctor, dentist or beautician. Keep a reading file handy for those times you are stuck in a line. Fill it with letters, memos, and magazine/newspaper articles you want to read.
5. Always call to confirm an appointment before you leave your home or office. This will ensure that the person you're meeting didn't forget about the appointment. Or, if that person is running late, you can do something else first.
6. Perform like tasks together. Make all your phone calls at once. Group errands by location and try to do them all at once. Or avoid errands by paying bills and shopping online. **PS:** Be prepared to run errands by keeping dry-cleaning, DVDs, library books, etc. in the car. If you happen to be driving past the establishment, you can stop.

7. Call before you make a trip to see if a store has a certain item. The clerk may even hold it for you. **PS:** Send gift certificates as presents. Phone in the order—no waiting in line, no crowded stores, and no having to wrap gifts.
8. Save time by withdrawing enough cash to last until your next paycheck. Stopping at the bank once every two weeks instead of twice a week can save you 19 hours a year!
9. Use a single calendaring system. Whether paper or palm, make it a simple master system which includes appointments, scheduled events and your "To Do" list.
10. Avoid telephone tag. If you must leave a message, make it detailed. Say why you called and when you can be reached, and speak slowly when leaving your phone number. Call service businesses, such as the phone company, on a Thursday or Friday. Their busiest days are Mondays and Tuesdays. Add regularly used phone numbers to your personal address book or, better yet, store them in speed dial.
    **PS:** Keep a simple project by the phone in case you're put on hold.
11. Save time at the video store by compiling a list of movies you want to see (keep it in that single calendaring system). Or just join Netflix!
12. Restrict TV viewing to shows that you value. Why not pay bills, clip coupons, mend, or iron while watching?

Bet you didn't know that October 24 is "Take Back Your Time" day. Based in Seattle, the Take Back Your Time (TBYT) organization (www.timeday.org) encourages people to challenge the epidemic of over-work, over-scheduling and time famine that now threatens our health, families and relationships, communities and environment.

# PLANES, TRAINS AND AUTOMOBILES

The U.S. has one of the stingiest vacation leave allotments in the industrialized world, so when it's time to hit the road, rails or skies you don't want to waste this precious time. You've earned it! I used these tips when I helped my client, Rick, get ready for a two-month stay in Bali. Whether you're heading to Wyoming for a week or Mexico for a month, the key is to plan ahead. Once you organize everything there's nothing left to do but have fun!

## ROAD TRIPS

1. Have each child pack a survival kit with games, coloring books, CDs, puzzles, etc. (This applies to any trip.) Make sure they avoid sharp objects like pens and pencils, since the slightest bump in the road could result in an injury. Crayons and markers are a better choice. Elmer's *Mess Free Go Paint!* (www.elmers.com; 800-848-9400) pen-brushes work only on accompanying special paper, so they won't stain upholstery or kids' skin and clothes. Turn your kids into happy, patient travelers with www.madallie.com; (877-462-3255), a children's online travel store. This site features the most creative toys, books, games, backpacks and more to keep kids occupied, and keep you sane, whenever you're on the road. **PS:** Cookie sheets and breakfast-in-bed trays are good flat surfaces for eating off, sticking magnetic toys to, and coloring.

2. Take a cooler packed with snacks, sandwiches and drinks and keep it in the car within easy reach. Don't forget napkins, tissues and wet wipes. And ladies, get some good roadmaps (men don't usually need them).

3. Maintenance is always less expensive than emergency road service so check the condition of tires, belts, battery, and spark plugs. Always keep an emergency kit in your car. This should include a flashlight, flares, tire changing tools, jumper cables, and a blanket.

## PLANE TRIPS

4. Avoid the busiest airports and the busiest times. The website of the National Air Traffic Controllers Association (www.natca.org) offers airport-specific reports on how to avoid delays. You can check the flights you're considering and see their record of on-time departures and cancellations at www.flightstats.com. If you want to check out

stats such as most delayed in departing/arriving airports, flights most often delayed, and airlines with the worst on-time track record, go to www.avoiddelays.com. It also gives near real-time flight reports and publishes last year's stats to help you avoid making the same mistake twice.

5. Use curbside checking, if available, and make sure cosmetics and other carry-on items conform to what the Transportation Security Administration dictates (www.tsa.gov).

6. Doesn't it seem that everyone's luggage is black? Tie a colored ribbon to your bags so you can easily spot them. Or have Sports Express (www.sportsexpress.com; 800-357-4174), Skycap International (www.skycapinternational.com; 877-775-9227), or Luggage Free (www.luggagefree.com; 800-361-6871), ship your bicycles, golf clubs, skis, and/or anything else you opt not to carry on your trip to your destination before you leave home.

7. Bring snacks, water, a book or magazine and a deck of cards to keep you busy during long airport waits. **PS:** Make sure your phone is fully charged.

8. Wear comfortable clothing and shoes. Carry an extra change of clothes in case you reach your final destination before your luggage does.

**ANY TRIP**

9. Gather legal or medical documents. Roll clothes into tight cylinders to save space. Pack breakables in the middle of your suitcase so your clothes will protect them. Pack a bag for dirty laundry and don't forget medications and a first aid kit.

10. In case of motion sickness, candied ginger appeals to kids. Fennel seed and peppermint teas help relieve nausea. Avoid eating greasy or salty foods before traveling; they can be hard to digest. Try a wrist bracelet that claims to cure nausea. There's no research that shows they work, but no harm in trying.

11. Before you head off, make sure things at home are in order. Leave numbers where you can be reached in case of emergency, stop newspaper and mail deliveries, toss or give away perishable food, take out the garbage, pay bills ahead that will come due while you're gone, arrange for pet care, and wash all dirty clothes. You're probably going to come home with dirty laundry so you don't want more greeting you when you arrive.

Baby's Away (www.babysaway.com) and Babies Travel Lite (www.babiestravellite.com; 888-450LITE) deliver clean, quality equipment such as car seats, cribs, high chairs, strollers, etc., for your children so that you can enjoy your stay while traveling.

And remember to leave extra space in your suitcase for souvenirs. Bon voyage!

# TOP-NOTCH TAG SALES

I have a prejudice. I admit it. I'm not a great fan of tag sales. To me they're a lot of work with very little monetary payoff. But Daniel Nissanoff, an online entrepreneur and author of *FutureShop*, estimates that most American homes have $2,200 worth of sellable stuff that isn't being used, so, what the heck, let's have a "tag," "yard," or "garage" sale! They are a great way to clear clutter, and can be a lot of fun. But you can't just drag stuff out of your garage, attic and basement and slap up a few signs. Here are eleven tips for the best ways to sell your castoffs:

1.  The most popular period for tag sales nationwide is between June and October. In college towns, the moving months of August and September can be particularly profitable. Dedicated shoppers get up early, so expect the biggest crowds at 8AM. Sundays are generally poor days for sales.

2.  Attracting buyers to the sale should be your top priority. But first make a call to town hall; some towns require a permit to hold a tag sale. Once you know the local rules, advertise in your daily newspaper (on Friday for a Saturday sale), as well as in a weekly newspaper in your area. **PS:** These websites offer free virtual bulletin boards for tag salers nationwide: www.craigslist.org, www.garagesalehunter.com, and www.yardsalesearch.com.

3.  Post large cardboard signs around the area and on main streets directing people to your house. Use black marker on a light colored background, big arrows, and the address so they can find your house easily. Use a single color of paperboard for all your signs so potential shoppers aren't confused by inconsistent signage.

4.  A yard sale with friends and neighbors will boost enthusiasm as well as help divide duties so the sale will run more smoothly, but keep in mind that having more sellers also requires more delegating and organizing, such as using different-colored price stickers for each seller. And since nothing attracts a crowd like a crowd, create an inviting party atmosphere by tying up balloons and playing music with mass appeal. Upbeat tunes are an instant people magnet at an outdoor sale. **PS:** Make sure you have someone on hand who can help move heavy objects or load items in buyers' cars.

5. Here's what you'll need to get rid of what you don't need: a fanny pack with lots of change; a calculator for tallying sales; measuring tape so shoppers can measure furniture; extension cords to test electrical appliances; a full-length mirror so shoppers can see what clothes look like; bubble wrap, boxes, and old newspapers for packing; and plastic bags to make it easy for shoppers to buy multiple items.

6. The top-selling tag sale items are: sports or soda memorabilia, such as old Coca-Cola or Pepsi bottles; collectibles such as vintage chrome appliances and Elvis mementos; DVDs and CDs; children's/baby clothes; classic toys; and decorative household items such as candleholders and lamps.

7. Create zones for the different kinds of items you're selling. Organize things into labeled sections, such as "housewares," "sports gear," "tools" and "kids." **PS:** Clean everything to make it look as new as possible.

8. Encourage browsing by setting up tables to form aisles so items are accessible from all sides. People backtrack a lot at yard sales, and you want to make it easy for them to return to things for a second look. How you display items can also work to your advantage. Put the most valuable items on tables so they can be more easily seen. Toys should be on the ground where kids can pick them up and get attached to them. Put big ticket items like furniture and electronics where drivers can see them.

9. Price it right. For a list of popular tag-sale items and suggested starting prices, go to www.realsimple.com/tagsale. Most tag-sale items usually end up selling for 10 percent of retail. Use removable stickers to price **everything**, no matter how small the item. **PS:** Be creative with pricing, like "buy one get one free," and don't be afraid to mark things down as the sale progresses.

10. Let's talk about men! They are a totally different type of tag-sale shopper. Even when just browsing, they shop with a goal in mind, and want to shop quickly. If you'll be offering tools or building supplies, put them up front where they'll be easily seen, and have an extension cord handy if anything is electric powered. **PS:** Items **must** be marked; many guys won't take the time to ask a price. Sort of how they won't ask for directions.

11. When the sale is over, don't take unsold items back to your house. Pack up what's left and donate to charity for a tax break.

When I helped my client, Randi, organize her tag sale she actually made about $500. But I can't take any of the credit; she had credible clutter.

*"Organizing is what you do before you do something, so that when you do it, it is not all mixed up."*

*A.A. Milne*

# MAKE YOUR NEXT MOVE A SANE MOVE

There's no way around it: moving stinks. It's often cited as one of the three most stressful life experiences. This reminds me of Linda's very funny story. Many years before, someone broke into her house, and when the police looked it over they told her the place had been ransacked. She told them it hadn't been; her house always looked like that! I guess no one would ever confuse Linda with Martha Stewart. When she hired me, the house was even more of a disaster because she had just sold it and was about to move. That's par for the course; moving is disruptive and chaotic. Over the years I've helped a lot of people, particularly seniors, move. The U.S. Census Bureau estimates that more than 43 million people move each year, with almost half packing up and relocating between Memorial Day and Labor Day. The following tips can help tame the chaos.

1.  If you don't use it, leave it. Packing for a move is a blessing in disguise. It's the perfect time to get rid of items that have collected in your home. Look at each item and think to yourself: "Do I use this? Do I need it?" Be honest. If you don't use/need an item give it away, sell it, or throw it away. **PS:** Some charities will pick up your donations.
2.  Consider hiring help. Sometimes it's best to leave the job to those who do it best: the professionals. Interview and get written estimates from at least three moving companies, and insist that a company rep visit the home rather than give a quote over the phone. Your best bet is to get recommendations from friends or a trusted real estate broker. **PS:** Go to www.protectyourmove.gov to file a complaint and/or check an interstate mover's registration status, insurance coverage and complaint history.
3.  Order plenty of packing supplies; don't skimp. Be sure to have lots of boxes, tape guns, tape, marking pens, bubble wrap, etc.
4.  Mark boxes clearly, and don't overfill them. Keep the weight of each box manageable so that one person can easily carry it without help. Mark boxes "HEAVY: BOOKS" to warn the box lifter. To avoid spills and breakage, write "FRAGILE" and "THIS END UP." Write the destination room and contents to make unpacking easier. **PS:** Pad items well, and consider drawing a diagram of the new house for the movers.

5. Take photos of cabinets and drawers in the old house so you'll be able to put things back the identical way when you unpack.

6. If you've hidden any valuables around the house, be sure to collect them before leaving. You should carry items such as jewelry with you, or keep them in a safe deposit box instead of packing them on the moving van.

7. Designate a central zone in the new house for the immediate necessities you'll need while you set up the other rooms.

8. Keep your workers happy and well-fueled. Have snacks ready for break time. Be sure to have plenty of beverages on hand, especially in warm weather. **PS:** Turn on heat or air conditioning to keep movers comfortable.

9. Make it easy for the movers to maneuver by clearing paths in the house and yard. If necessary, take down stairwell handrails, trim bushes and trees, and prop open gates to aid access. Make sure to tie up the dog, and keep the kids and toys clear of the movers' path.

10. Remember to leave out cleaning supplies for the final once-over before closing the door for good. **PS:** Vacuum furniture before moving day. It's more pleasant to move a chair or couch that isn't dusty or covered with animal hair.

11. Keep your pets' routines as regular as possible as you prepare to move. During the final crunch, keep them at a friend's house or a kennel, reducing the chance of Fido or Fluffy getting upset and running away. Keep some form of identification on the pet at all times. **PS:** Moving companies usually cannot transport animals or plants. Plan ahead and make arrangements for their safe transfer.

12. Don't forget spare house keys. Whether it means retrieving them from neighbors or from under the rock next to the front door, make sure to gather all sets before your final departure.

13. Check the nooks and crannies. Take one last look through the drawers and cabinets, wipe all surfaces and clean out crumbs as a courtesy to the people moving in, and be sure you haven't left anything of value behind. **PS:** Make sure to leave the garage door opener for the new residents.

And don't forget to submit a change of address form. Good luck!

# A "BREATHE-EASY" HOLIDAY

Allison had four Christmas trees! One home; four trees! She was a frazzled wreck when she called me; determined to have one of those holidays that exist only in the pages of lavish shelter magazines. She was trying to decorate, bake the perfect cookies for Santa, shop, plan her annual holiday party, and wrap presents all at the same time. Talk about juggling a lot of balls.

Ah, the holidays. Time off to spend with family and friends, food and drink, comforting surroundings, warmth, joy and goodwill, right? So why are so many of us stressed, depressed and exhausted? It's really hard to not get caught up in the trappings of the holidays and, before you know it, you're feeling like a stressed-out Scrooge. Try sailing through the season with these suggestions.

**FIRST THINGS FIRST**
1. Whatever holiday you celebrate, maintain a realistic notion about what that holiday should be; don't get so caught up in the planning that you forget to enjoy the season. Remember, less than perfect is perfectly okay.
2. Check out www.organizedchristmas.com. Their mission (and you should choose to accept it), is to help you get organized for a stress-free holiday.

**GIFTS/SHOPPING**
3. Check out www.presentpicker.com (888-860-0145) if you need some gift-giving inspiration. This site will suggest items after you've plugged in the recipient's age, gender, personality, occupation, interests and lifestyle. **PS:** Consider giving the gift of "doing." Go to www.xperiencedays.com, which offers activities like hot-air ballooning, drag racing, and cooking classes.
4. Shop early for presents, party supplies, and decorations. Buy multiples of gift tags, tape and wrappings; you can always use the leftovers next year. Keep a stash of "one-size-fits-all" gifts like wine and candy on hand in case you need a last-minute present.
5. Avoid crowded malls by shopping in small neighborhood stores, which usually have more one-of-a-kind gifts. If you must tackle the mall, go at off times (dinner hour, weekdays) and leave the kids at

home. Or shop from mail-order catalogs and the Internet or give gift certificates.

6. How about a personalized, one-of-a-kind present for grandma and grandpa? Check out www.personalcreations.com (888-527-1404) for calendars, quilts, computer mouse pads, mugs, and ties customized with pix of the grandchildren.

7. The right gifts are just as welcome in simple packages. Choose only a couple of wrapping paper designs, one for adults and one for kids. Or just use gift bags or decorative boxes.

8. Take advantage if a store offers free gift-wrapping or seek out charity gift-wrapping services; you'll be contributing to a worthy cause.

9. The commercialized holiday culture encourages everyone to focus on getting lots of stuff. But many religious traditions instruct us that true joy and purpose come from focusing on the needs of others. So why not pick the perfect present and help a worthy cause? At Presents for Purpose (www.presentsforpurpose.com; 212-580-0515), up to 25 percent of the sale price of the apparel, watches, jewelry, accessories and gifts go to partner charities. Women for Women International (www.womenforwomen.org; 202-737-7705) helps women in war-torn countries with job-skills training, and educational and financial support. At The Appreciate Network (www.appreciate.org; 866-718-1005), you can get gorgeous organic holiday gifts and baskets filled with socially responsible brands such as Newman's Own Organics, Burt's Bees, Green Mountain Coffee Roasters, etc. The National Arbor Day Foundation's (www.arborday.org; 888-448-7337) "Trees in Celebration" program plants Lodgepole pine and Douglas fir trees in national forests which have been destroyed by fire, disease or insects. For each $10 donated, ten trees will be planted; you receive a certificate which you can send or personally present to the person you have chosen to honor. Consider becoming a Philanthropreneur, a person who uses the skills of an entrepreneur to advance the goals of a philanthropist. A nonprofit group called Charity Checks (www.charitychecks.us; 800-854-5601) offers giving certificates which allow the recipients to make a donation to the charity of their choice. The recipient chooses the charity and the donor gets the tax deduction.

## FINANCIAL

10. Avoid the shock of a hefty January credit card bill by making a budget and sticking to it! Catalog/online shopping can help; you won't be seduced at the local mall by a million choices staring you in the face.

11. Remember cash? It may be tough to use when you're making so many purchases; credit and debit cards are more convenient. But if you really want to guarantee you'll spend within your means, use real money.

12. Save your receipts. Gather them up at the end of a shopping day and put them somewhere for safekeeping. Before you wrap gifts, review how much you spent and, if you're over budget, decide which to return. It's much easier to make this decision with all the gifts in front of you.

## DECORATING/ENTERTAINING

13. Send holiday invites at least a month in advance, if only in the form of save-the-date announcements. Reserve rental equipment as early as you can. Book help—babysitters, caterers, musicians—as far in advance as possible.

14. Do you dread the food preparation that goes along with entertaining? Don't feel the need to make everything from scratch. Buy vegetables pre-chopped and other ingredients partially prepared. You can pick up wonderful side dishes from the deli section of your grocery store or specialty shop and, if you serve them in your own bowl or platter, no one will know the difference. Stick with recipes that don't involve 75 different steps, and choose the ones that you can easily time so they all finish cooking at once. And do not, under any circumstances, try new recipes on party day! Better to keep things simple, and use tried-and-true favorites. You may have eaten that pork tenderloin 110 times, but it will be new to your guests.

15. Try to space food and drink so there isn't a traffic jam around one table or in one room. Spread things out, and everyone will be more comfortable. **PS:** Forego a full bar; it's too much of a hassle, unless you're hiring a bartender. Try a wine (or beer, martini, smoothie, etc.) sampling station. This gives guests an opportunity to try different types of drinks.

16. Know when to politely say no to invitations. Decide which gatherings you must attend and which can be skipped without guilt. Only say yes to meaningful events.
17. Decorate as your time and inclination call for, and let it go at that. One stunning wreath on your front door may be all you need. Or decorate only the room your family uses most often.

## COOKING/BAKING
18. Words that strike fear in a mother's heart: "Mom, I told my teacher I'd bring cookies tomorrow." Have several packs of refrigerated cookie dough on hand.
19. Keep a special notebook of holiday recipes you would like to make year after year. This will save a lot of time searching through cookbooks. You can store your holiday notebook with your other recipes (if you might want to use it at other times during the year), or in with your decorations.

## PERSONAL
20. Choose some special holiday looks from your closet(s) and make sure they're ready to wear. Find some festive items in each person's closet ahead of time to avoid last-minute stress.
21. Treat yourself with respect by setting aside special "you time." Unwind with a friend, get a manicure, go to a matinee, or spend an afternoon alone. You'll feel reenergized.

## LAST BUT NOT LEAST
22. Avoid long lines at the post office by using Automated Postal Centers, the Postal Service's version of an ATM. APCs provide a quick, easy and convenient way for customers to weigh, calculate and apply exact postage, and ship Express Mail and Priority Mail items, packages and First-Class letters right at the kiosks. They also provide easy access to postal products and services the same way ATMs provide access to banking services. The kiosks accept debit and credit cards and don't charge a service fee.
23. Skip holiday cards to anyone you haven't seen or heard from in over a year, or just send New Year's cards in January. You can spend more time on personal messages and recipients will have more time to read them.

24. Shift the emphasis from consumerism to togetherness by focusing on family activities. Share special moments like a holiday show, fancy brunch or holiday trip instead of spending money on piles of gifts.
25. Give to the less fortunate as part of your holiday tradition. Volunteer at a homeless shelter, visit a retirement center or participate in a food, toy or clothing drive. Encourage kids to give away toys they no longer use.

So relax, have fun, enjoy the holiday, and focus on the people you love. That's the "stuff" that really matters.

*"Unnecessary possessions are unnecessary burdens. If you have them, you have to take care of them! There is great freedom in simplicity of living. It is those who have enough but not too much who are the happiest."*

Peace Pilgrim

# ARE YOU READY FOR ANYTHING?

Disasters can range from inconvenient to devastating and, luckily for my client Lillian, a small kitchen fire was more the former than the latter. An earthquake, flood, tornado, fire or terrorist event can happen anytime, anywhere. Any of these things may cause you to lose utilities — gas, water, electricity — or the ability to communicate with others. You may not have to actually leave your home, but it's still important to have enough to survive. In a national survey, only 37 percent of Americans said they have a family communications plan in the event of an emergency. Just over half (53 percent) said they have a designated emergency contact person, but only 28 percent have an agreed-upon location to meet family members in case local communication is impossible. Yes, I know it's hard to prepare for a catastrophe that may not happen soon, or at all, but all of us need to prepare for the unexpected. These eleven tips will help.

1. Prepare a Disaster Supplies Kit with 72 hours' worth of supplies, including:
   - a gallon of water per person per day
   - non perishable food
   - change of clothing, including hats, gloves, rain gear, and sturdy footwear
   - blanket or sleeping bag
   - toilet articles: toothbrush, toothpaste, soap, toilet paper, contact lenses and supplies
   - flashlight and extra batteries (don't include candles; they cause more fires after a disaster than anything else)
   - medical needs: insulin, prescription drugs, extra eyeglasses, heart and high blood pressure medication
   - paper plates, cups and plastic utensils
   - matches in a waterproof container
   - non-electric can opener and utility knife
   - radio with batteries (check often to make sure batteries are still good)
   - soap, liquid detergent, disinfectant, hand sanitizer and bleach
   - scissors, duct tape
   - special items for infants, disabled or elderly family members
   - extra set of car keys

Your kit should be in an easy-to-carry container such as a backpack or duffle bag. Store it in a convenient place known by all family members. Remember to review your kit once a year and update water, food, and batteries as they become outdated. **PS:** The Red Cross offers a variety of Emergency Preparedness kits and supplies ([www.redcross.org](www.redcross.org); 800-REDCROSS).

2. Prepare an Emergency Car Kit which includes
   - blanket
   - booster cables
   - maps, shovels, and flares
   - tire repair kit and pump
   - fire extinguisher
   - battery-powered radio, flashlight and extra batteries
   - first aid kit
   - fire extinguisher (5 lb., A-B-C type)

3. Make a family communications plan. If your family knows where to go and what to do in an emergency, they'll save time and remain calm. Your plan should contain:
   - the name and phone number of out-of-state relatives to contact (long distance calling may be easier than local calling)
   - two family meeting places, the first at a designated spot (a tree or other prominent landmark) outside your home, and the second a designated location outside your neighborhood in case you cannot return home
   - a home evacuation route with at least two ways out of each room
   - a designated room in your house in case authorities instruct you to "shelter in place"

4. Compile a master list of names, addresses and phone numbers of friends, relatives, physicians, attorneys, insurance agents, bankers, etc. If possible, include cell phone, email and beeper information. Update it regularly and give one to every family member. **PS:** Post emergency numbers by all phones and make sure all children can dial 9-1-1 in case of emergency.

5. Keep about $500 in cash on hand in small bills. When the power goes out, so do ATMs. Store a roll of quarters in the trunk of your car in case you need to make an emergency phone call after your cell phone stops working. During the aftermath of Hurricane Katrina,

Wal-Mart allowed those who had cash to buy off the shelf. With no electricity or phone lines, stores can't process credit cards.

6. Prepare a "Grab-and-Go" case that is fireproof, lockable, and light enough to carry in an emergency. Keep all important documents in this box, including that $500 or travelers checks. Include financial account numbers, deeds, titles, wills, insurance policies, stocks and bonds, passports, Social Security cards, driver's licenses, and birth, death and marriage certificates. **PS:** The best way to protect documents is to put them on a U.S.B. flash drive and give it to a friend or trusted family member who does not live near you.

7. Prepare a household inventory — a written list, photos or video — of your home and belongings. Remember to store the inventory somewhere other than your home.

8. Keep your insurance up to date. With homes appreciating in value, you may also find you need to increase coverage. If you're a renter, buy renters insurance.

9. When asked what they regret losing most, people almost always say photos. Consider scanning old photos to your computer and putting them on a disk. If you're faced with disaster, the originals may be destroyed, but you've got a better chance of the disk surviving, and it will also take up less space. **PS:** Free online photo services like www.flickr.com, www.snapfish.com, or www.kodakgallery.com allow you to upload photos to the internet so you can access them from any computer.

10. Familiarize family members with fire extinguisher locations and teach them how to use a fire extinguisher using the PASS method: Pull the pin, Aim at the base of the flames, Squeeze the trigger, Sweep back and forth along the flames.

11. Pets are family members, too. Make sure dogs and cats are wearing collars and up-to-date identification. Don't forget your pet's vaccination records, medication, and leash, harness or carrier, and a two- to three-day supply of food. **PS:** Have a safe place to take your pets if possible; most disaster shelters can't accept pets.

For more information on emergency preparedness visit www.ready.gov, or call 800-237-3239 for a free brochure.

*"You can't have everything...*
*Where would you put it?"*

*Steven Wright*

# HELP! I WANT TO GET OFF THE LIST!

We each get about 560 pieces of junk mail annually — a waste of both time and paper. Take 15 minutes today to stop the flow of unwanted junk mail (and calls).

1. The Direct Marketing Association will put your name on a "do not mail" list, which all its members must cross-reference before sending a solicitation. Go to www.dmaconsumers.org/cgi/offmailinglist or write to

   Direct Marketing Association
   Mail Preference Service
   P.O. Box 9008
   Farmingdale, NY 11735-9008

   Include your complete name, address, and ZIP code, and state that you wish to "activate the preference service." This should stop about 75 percent of the junk mail you currently receive.
2. Always write "no mailing lists" on any product warranties/rebates you send in.
3. The Consumer Credit Reporting Industry will remove your name from the mailing lists that credit card companies use to send out offers. Go to www.optoutprescreen.com or call 888-5OPTOUT.
4. This site has a host of other anti-junk mail links and tips: www.nativeforest.org/stop_junk_mail
5. To decrease the amount of unsolicited telemarketing calls you receive, register with the Federal Trade Commission's National Do Not Call Registry at www.donotcall.gov, or call 888-382-1222. This toll-free number also applies to cell phones, but you must call from the cell number you want to block. Don't call from a different phone number. Companies who ignore the Registry face fines of up to $11,000 per violation. **PS:** Your registration will not expire. The Federal Trade Commission will not drop any telephone numbers from the National Do Not Call Registry based on a five-year expiration period pending final Congressional or agency action on whether to make registration permanent.

*"True contentment is not in having everything, but in being satisfied with everything you have."*

*Anonymous*

# CLUTTER FOR A CAUSE

## ANYTHING AND EVERYTHING
AmVets
www.amvets.org
800-810-7148
Founded to assist American veterans and their dependents, AmVets accepts practically anything.

Excess Access
www.excessaccess.com
415-242-6041
An online system that matches business and household items with nearby nonprofits and recyclers.

## BARTERING/CONNECTING WITH OTHERS
Craig's List
www.craigslist.org
This site will connect you with other buyers in your area. Just click on the city nearest you and then the "for sale" section.

Freecycle
www.freecycle.org
The Freecycle Network connects you with people who are giving, and getting, stuff for free in their own towns.

Live Deal
www.livedeal.com
A website-selling tool where you can sell just about anything. Postings connect shoppers and buyers who are within driving distance of each other.

Swap-Bot
www.swap-bot.com
This site organizes swaps among folks who want to trade hand-assembled items through the postal mail. Items can include mix CDs, postcards, crafts, or anything you can think of!

## BATTERIES

Rechargeable Battery Recycling Corporation
www.rbrc.org and/or www.call2recycle.org
800-8-BATTERY
Can help you recycle used portable rechargeable batteries. There are more than 30,000 drop-off sites in the United States, including Radio Shack, Home Depot, Staples and other retail outlets. Common alkaline batteries used in toys and flashlights CAN be thrown in the trash as they don't contain any mercury. **PS:** Service stations are required to take back automotive lead acid batteries.

## BICYCLES

Pedals for Progress
www.p4p.org
908-638-4811
Donates bicycles (and sewing machines) to partner charities in 28 countries.

## BOOKS

Books for Soldiers
www.booksforsoldiers.com
Soldiers (and Sailors, Marines, etc.) make requests in an online forum; you send literary care packages directly to them.

International Book Project
www.intlbookproject.org
This nonprofit humanitarian group has been sending books to orphanages, schools, and churches worldwide for over 40 years.

Reader to Reader
www.readertoreader.org
413-256-8595
Children's and teen titles are in highest demand. They must be in good shape and suitable for pre-K to high school students.

To cut down on shipping, send books via media mail at the U.S. Post Office.

## BOOK-SWAP
Bookins
www.bookins.com
Provides postage, tracks all shipments, and will even pick up the cost of sending a replacement for lost or damaged shipments.

PaperBackSwap
www.paperbackswap.com
678-802-1922
Readers share books with each other (NOT just paperbacks) for nothing more than the cost of postage.

Readers United
www.readersunited.com
When you send a book to somebody you are awarded credits when it arrives. You then use those credits to request books from other members on the site. Members send books directly to each other.

## CELL PHONES
Cingular
www.cingular.com
888-333-6651
Through the Cingular Wireless Reuse & Recycle program, consumers bring unwanted wireless phones, PDAs, accessories and batteries (regardless of the manufacturer or carrier) to Cingular Wireless operated stores and participating authorized dealer stores for recycling.

Sprint
www.sprint.com
800-SPRINT1
Sprint Project Connect accepts all makes and models of phones, regardless of service provider. To recycle a phone, pick up a postage-paid envelope at any participating Sprint store nationwide. Or, print the postage-paid mailing label available on their website. Net proceeds from Sprint Project Connect go to benefit K-12 education programs.

Staples
www.staples.com
800-3STAPLE
Offers a nationwide Mobile Devices Recycling program for recycling used cell phones, PDAs, pagers and rechargeable batteries. Customers can drop them off at their local Staples store. A large portion of the proceeds generated from recycling the mobile electronics devices is donated to the Sierra Club.

Verizon Wireless
www.verizonwireless.com
800-922-0204
Verizon's HopeLine Phone Recycling Program uses refurbished and recycled wireless equipment and Verizon Wireless services to assist victims of domestic violence.

## CLOTHING
Clothes Make the Man Program
www.cmtm.org
860-293-2909
Provides suitable interview and employment attire for low-income men.

Dress for Success
www.dressforsuccess.org
212.532.1922
Provides work-appropriate clothing to low-income women who can't afford the wardrobe necessary to land a job.

One Warm Coat
www.onewarmcoat.org
877-663-9276
Helps to redistribute tens of thousands of coats in the communities where they are originally donated. Check out the interactive map on their website to see if there is a coat drive scheduled near you. If nothing is listed, check back for updates or consider holding your own donation event.

**COMPUTERS, ETC.**
Apple, Dell, Gateway, HP, and IBM all have take-back programs.

To find a company that'll refurbish your high-tech stuff (computers, monitors, printers, etc.) for nonprofits in need, or junk it without hurting the neighborhood, go to www.techsoup.org/recycle/donate. You may have to pay a small fee ($5 to $20) to have stuff picked up.

If you have a computer, printer, scanner, or monitor to donate, check out the World Computer Exchange at www.worldcomputerexchange.org.

National Cristina Foundation
www.cristina.org
203-863-9100
Donors fill out a simple form on its Web site and the organization searches for a request from a local nonprofit, school or public agency looking for equipment that matches your old computer, laptop or printer. Once a match is made, usually within two weeks of listing your donation, the donor and recipient can arrange for a drop-off or pickup of the equipment.

Technical Stuff
1. Donate unwanted floppies to Floppies for Kiddies. Learn more by calling 504-898-2158. To mail, send to Floppies for Kiddies, 20349 Highway 36, Covington, LA 70433
2. Compact computer disks and audio CDs may be recycled through NE-SAR Systems. For shipping instructions and package weight limits, contact NE-SAR at 724-827-8172, or write to NE-SAR Systems, 420 Ashwood Road, Darlington, PA 16115-9325.

**EYEGLASSES**
Give the Gift of Sight
www.givethegiftofsight.com
513-765-6000
Drop them off at any LensCrafters, Pearle Vision, Sears Optical, Target Optical, BJ's Optical, Sunglass Hut or Lions Club location. After cleaning the glasses, they will send them to poor and developing countries such as Honduras or Ecuador. The glasses are paired up with people in need who have similar prescriptions.

New Eyes for the Needy
www.neweyesfortheneedy.org
973-376-4903
This organization accepts metal frames in any condition, unbroken
plastic-frame glasses, sunglasses, hearing aids, and cataract lenses. It
also accepts jewelry and giftware, which are sold to raise money for
glasses.

## HEARING AIDS
Hear Now
www.sotheworldmayhear.org
866-354-3254
Part of the Starkey Hearing Foundation, Hear Now repairs and resells
donated hearing aids. They deliver more than 20,000 hearing aids
annually through more than 100 hearing missions a year in countries
stretching from the U.S. to Vietnam.

Many service organizations, including The Lions Clubs and Knights of
Columbus, run hearing aid banks and other hearing aid recycling
programs.

## JUNK REMOVAL
1-800-GOT-JUNK
www.1800gotjunk.com
800-GOT-JUNK
North America's largest junk removal service. They do all the loading
into their truck, and then your junk is recycled, taken to a transfer
station, or sent to a landfill. Pricing is based on your city, volume, and
the nature of your material. They'll take construction materials, garden
refuse, furniture, appliances, and other items. No hazardous waste
accepted.

1-800-PACK-RAT
www.1800packrat.com
800-PACK-RAT
Offers portable storage for all your storage and moving needs. PACK-
RAT portable storage units are secure, all-steel and weatherproof, and
their facilities are 100% secure and climate-controlled.

## MUSICAL INSTRUMENTS

Hungry for Music

www.hungryformusic.org

202-479-2810

Hungry for Music's mission is to inspire underprivileged children (and others) by bringing positive musical and creative experiences into their lives. Since becoming a non-profit in 1994, Hungry for Music has brought the healing quality of music to thousands of people through its musical instrument donations, concerts, and workshops.

## SCHOOL EQUIPMENT

I Love Schools

www.iloveschools.com

I Love Schools matches teachers with donors of equipment, supplies and materials.

## SPORTS EQUIPMENT

Nike Go Campaign

www.nikego.com

This is a national program to help increase the quality and quantity of P.E. in schools where it has been reduced or eliminated. Nike Go recycles all brands of athletic shoes to create premium sport surfaces such as football fields, tracks, basketball courts, and tennis courts.

Sports Gift Inc.

www.sportsgift.org

949-388-2359

Sports Gift is focused on providing sports to underprivileged children throughout the world and promoting sports related community service among our youth.

And don't forget the old standbys: churches, schools, community centers, Goodwill and the Salvation Army. Your generosity is likely to be a tax write-off.

*"Our houses are such unwieldy property that we are often imprisoned rather than housed in them."*

*Henry David Thoreau*

# IT'S BAAACK!

If I have a client for years, I've done something wrong. A good organizer teaches how to get, and stay, organized. I always tell clients that unless I move in with them (some have certainly wanted me to), they have to maintain their wonderful new organizing systems. That doesn't mean that Lucie, Gladys and Shirley won't call for periodic maintenance. Some backsliding is par for the course. It's like when you've been doing well on a diet, so you decide it's time for a hot fudge sundae. But the next day you go back to healthy eating. Organizing is like that. It's a journey; an ongoing process. Sometimes when I'm really busy, I'll leave stuff around for a few days, but only a few days. That way it doesn't get over-whelming. If you allow that one magazine to sit on the kitchen counter for a week, it seems to attract other magazines. Before you know it, you're back to square one. Consider the following:

1. When you first de-cluttered it probably felt great to have so much more time and energy. Try to remember that feeling and you'll be less likely to backslide.
2. Organizing may mean committing to, and perhaps tweaking, a new daily routine. Are you more efficient if you go to bed a half hour earlier and wake up a half hour earlier? Maybe laying out your clothes the night before makes sense. Or putting lunches together the night before. As you tweak, look back and reflect on which strategies made the most difference to your day.
3. Remember, clutter is postponed decisions, so don't procrastinate (reread pages 11-13). Once everything has a home, try to return things to their designated spots as soon as you can. Deal with each item when it appears — either put it away or throw it away — then clutter can't come back. This could take as little as five minutes at the end of each day.
4. Try not to let those pesky paper piles start to grow on horizontal surfaces. But if they do, turn the pile over and sort from the bottom. That's where the older stuff is. You've learned to live without it for awhile and can more easily throw it away.

Doing these 13 simple things will prevent a relapse:

Use it, **put it back**
Read it, **return it**
Listen to it, **put it back**
Open it, use it, **throw it away**
Bring it home, **put it in its place**
Borrow it, **return it**
Play with it, **put it away**
Drive/ride it, **put it in the garage**
Bounce it, **put it away**
Take them off, **put them on the shoe rack**
Wear it, **put it in the hamper or closet**
Dry off with it, **hang it on a towel rack**
Buy it, bring it home, **find a place for it**

Remember, organizing isn't rocket science. Five minutes a day can make all the difference. You **can** do it!

## About Rosemary:

I never knew what I wanted to be when I grew up. I would get a job, master it, get bored, and quit. Over and over again. I always thought there had to be something more than 9 to 5 and an eventual gold watch. Work was a necessary evil; something I fit in between all the fun things I really wanted to be doing. It never, ever occurred to me that it could be fulfilling; something I could love.

When I moved in the mid 90s, I became completely immersed in organizing my new home. Days went by; I barely got tired or hungry. I achieved "flow" — the mental state in which a person is fully immersed in what he or she is doing, characterized by feelings of energy, focus and full involvement.

Ever so slowly it dawned on me that I loved to make order out of chaos. In 1999, I decided to turn this talent/skill into a profession. What the heck, I figured I could always go back and get a "normal" job. At last I'd figured out what I wanted to be when I grew up — better late than never! And, since "organizing" is an enormous umbrella that covers so many different topics, I never get bored. I love helping others and truly believe I make a difference in clients' lives. And, luckily, there's plenty of chaos for me to organize!

## About Ernie:

Ernie Conte, a graduate of Paier School of Art, has been a freelance illustrator, cartoonist, and graphic designer for 30 years. He was a staff artist and art director at Lender's Bagels, a national food company. His humorous illustrations have appeared in magazines, newspapers, posters, menus, greeting cards, and other advertising vehicles around the country.

Rosemay is passionate about the benefits of an organized lifestyle, and she'd like to organize the world; one person at a time, one organization at a time.

Is this the year you're going to get organized? How can Rosemary help?

**WE WOULD LOVE TO HEAR FROM YOU!**

Ideas, comments, suggestions? Feel free to email Rosemary at **rosemary@borntoorganize.com.** And please check out her website: www.borntoorganize.com.

If you would like to schedule Rosemary for a meeting or speaking engagement, or make a bulk discount purchase of *Clutter, Chaos & the Cure*, contact Rosemary's agent/publisher, Eitan Battat. He can be reached at 866-836-7913, or go to www.kiwipublishing.com.

**KIWI Publishing, Inc.**
**P.O. Box 3852**
**Woodbridge, CT 06525.**

# REVIEWS FROM WWW.AMAZON.COM

"This book is an easy and fun read — great illustrations, organizing tips and ideas. It also has fun facts/trivia, like how the U.S. has more malls than high schools. This book is well worth the price and should easily help one get organized "!

*An East Coast Girl*

"As a chronic pack rat and the owner of three other books on organizing, totaling 697 pages, I was delighted to come across this handy little volume. In a mere 98 pages, "Clutter, Chaos & the Cure" cuts right to the chase, telling you all you need to know to make getting organized easy, fun and so rewarding. The author has a great sense of humor, understands the psychology of clutterers, and offers a multitude of valuable, easy-to follow hints. Her top five organizing tips, on one and a half pages, are worth buying the book! I refer back to them constantly. Even the illustrations amuse. Highly recommended"!

*Ro-bee, "Messy No More"*

"I found this book to be witty and fun with soooo many great tips I never would have thought of! A must read for everyone."

*T. Challey*

"This book taught me a lot. Two of the most useful chapters were 'Clutter for a Cause,' which advises the reader where to donate just about anything, and 'It's Baaack'!, which addresses relapses. And everyone will recognize themselves in the chapter called 'Sound Familiar.' All in all, an easy-to-read, fun book that supplies a spoonful of sugar to make the organizing medicine go down. "

*Dee Lowell, "Tranquility Seeker"*

"Love this book! It's breezy and easy-to-read. The suggestions are simple, yet things I never thought of or have not thought of in ages. Read this book; it is a must-have and a great, great gift for the person who has everything but organization. "

*The Idea Chick*

"If you want to get smart about organizing your personal and professional lives, this is the book to read."

*Jay Robert Guy*

"I am so impressed with this book! I've got several others on the same subject, but this one is the most comprehensive and to-the-point. It's also chock-full of helpful hints. I loved the resources--from where to purchase good items for organizing to where to donate/get rid of things. It's definitely worth the price, and Ernie Conte's illustrations are an added bonus."

*Berkeley Barb, "Daydream Believer"*

"Great book. Easy-to-read, not overwhelming; short chapters; clever wit."

*I.M. Ahoarder, "Pack Mouse"*

"Your book has brought much joy to me and my children. I am applying your suggestions and am slowly but steadily getting my house in order. It has made my project more manageable. I thank you for your efforts in writing it. You did a fantastic job. I will recommend it to others."

*Catherine M. Beebe*
*www.homereferralsourcect.com*

*"Organization is the key to success with anything."*

*Scott Bilker*